The 4 Principles of Coaching Dreams Into Success

It's so basic — It's Brilliant!

Coach Don White

Thoughts
Developed

Acknowledgement

A host of people have assisted along my journey of crafting *Coaching Dreams Into Success*. I am confident that I will unintentionally omit a person or more. Please know in my heart that your contribution is worth its weight in gold to me. People have contributed various types of resources, friendship, a listening ear, staunch feedback, emotional support, critical thinking suggestions, mentoring, coaching and love. I am and will remain forever humbly grateful for everyone.

One person in particular that I must recognize first and foremost is my beautiful wife Alisa Williams. You have provided me all the support and more than I could ever hope for. I am extremely grateful and appreciative to have you by my side, as we say "wearing the jersey." I love you and thank you profusely.

Thank you Medina (Mom), Charles (Dad), Shirl (Mom), Aunt Jenny (Mom), Daddy George (Pops), Cindy Singletary, Verline Dotson, Willie Hill, Ralph Armstrong, Jabril, Arlene Selis Karpas, Mike Gottfried, Green Sweater Man, Tony Etter, Maurice "Mo," Ralph Lee, Muhammad, Pam and Richard Bailey, Jackie Etter, Billie Hackett, Ronald, Ken and Scott Blanchard, Trevor Otts, Che Brown, Rick and Odessa Hopkins, Cynthia Hawkins, Edward Harper, Adrian Rias, Don Becker, Bill Breetz, Dick Seitz, Dave Kavenaugh, Lynn and Darrell Calloway, Sharon, Donna, Leah, Yvonne Ruffin, Diane Lewis,

My Racer Teammates, Mohammad, Stu Horton, Bernard and Alicia Smith, Bob Kelly, Graylyn Swilley-Woods, Dr. George C. Fraser, Moach, Kendall, Cynthia Jane Evans, Ron Martin, Gerald "6'9," Ann and Herbert Green, Holly Terry, Ron Zook, Frank Beamer, Jeff "Gump," Terry and Michelle Lancaster, Carole Conlon, Nate Lett, Damon Evans, Joe Buddy, Jim Berger, Richard Layson, Charlie Phillips, Forest Park Auto Shop, Bill Kelly, Mrs. Donaldson, Rodney "Rock," Kenny "KD," Eric Ellis, Vincent Jones, Randy and Bonita Billingsley, Marcus "MJ," Willie "Still Will," Terrell Griffin, Lila Talbott, Shawna, and the Miami Football Birthday Crew. To my aunts, uncles, cousins, nieces, nephews and adorable grandchildren. A special shout out to my children Omar, Donielle, Chris and daughter-in-law Arion. To all the Glory and Praise I submit to my Lord, the one and only God.

Table of Contents

INTRODUCTION

Do you strive to be a high performer, to increase your production, or simply to be able to relax without stress? From time to time everyone is confronted with a situation when they do not have enough time or resources in a day. Some people struggle with clarity and focus. Others scratch their head when it comes to developing an effective and efficient way of working to achieve results at the highest level. What's tough is knowing how to selflessly, but with bravado, distinguish oneself as the go-to person or subject matter expert.

Coaching Dreams Into Success (CDIS) provides you with solutions to live your best life, build stronger relationships, make more money, develop better habits, and produce with greater efficiency and effectiveness. CDIS focuses on four of life's most important principles: Balance, Vision, Strategy and Branding. Each principle is supported with a proven step-by-step process. The CDIS principles have stood the test of time. The principles cross cultural boundaries, help individuals cut through mediocrity, serve as a call to action, and lead to inspiring and enhancing **greatness** and **success**.

I have learned that you define your own greatness and success. You define your greatness and success by putting in the work. Just as important as putting in the work, it is your methods, tools and strategy for putting in the work that will result in your ability to achieve greatness and success. For over four decades, I have studied leadership development and provided platform training for organizations across the United States. My experiences have taught me many valuable life lessons, some of which I will share with you in this book.

As a college student athlete on a football scholarship who aspired to be great and not to fall into the dumb jock mold, I almost flunked out of Murray State University. The pretty girls, shooting pool and playing football received most of my time. Sadly, I put class toward the bottom of my list of priorities.

After receiving a report card that had a message on the bottom reading, "As of this notice you are immediately on academic probation," I went to see the academic advisor. She asked me what my major was, and I replied Business Economics. She then asked me if I had a course curriculum, to which I replied no. How was I ever to be great if I had no plan?

To make a long story short, the advisor gave me a course curriculum and a highlighter. She told me that if I wanted to graduate, I needed to guard the book and highlighter with my life. From that point forward, I was equipped and ready to go. I refocused my vision, redirected my energy and balanced my priorities, leading me to graduate with my Bachelor of Science in Occupational Safety and Health Engineering. In addition to my academic achievement, on the football team I earned two tackling records, first team ALL-OVC, and three-time OVC Conference Player of the Week.

I learned my lesson early: "You have to do what you *need* to do in order to do what you *want* to do."

After visiting with the advisor, I sat on a bench and began to process different life scenarios. Bottom line was that I defined my "Why," which was to get my degree and play football. I have always thought that earning my degree and being an accomplished athlete would help propel me to be recognized as a thought leader; this is my greatness. I defined my greatness and success back then and have been carrying it with me ever since.

The lesson my college advisor gave me was captured in a phrase I heard Dr. George Fraser say at a business conference in Dallas, Texas. According to Dr. Fraser, "If you want to live a good life, you will have to perform at a level of greatness. If you want to live a great life, you will have to perform at a level of excellence. If you want to live an excellent life, you will have to perform at a level of being extraordinary."

We all have *wills* and *wants* that drive us like no other motivation. Your *will* is expressed by your words of conviction to action. Your *want* is your intentional physical act of fulfilling your conviction without reservation to pursue your aim. There is nothing that can suppress your will and want. Only you can suppress your will and want. The benefits you receive in life are the residual of your work. Are you ready?

This is your personal book to read, practice strategies, and take on experiential challenges. You will also find inspirational quotes and learning nuggets. As you read and work your way through the CDIS principles, you will have an opportunity to discover your "Why," determine your Core Values, define your Vision, adopt a global Strategy, and develop your Brand.

The power behind the effectiveness of CDIS is my signature three-pronged approach:

1. Content delivery is C3 (Clear, Concise and Compelling)

2. Processes are easy to follow

3. Helpful tools allow you to connect to your "Why"

Thank you for adding this book to your library. Please tell your family and friends about CDIS to help share this information with others so they can make better decisions to improve the quality of their personal and professional lives. This is my mission.

CHAPTER 1

INSPIRATION

I believe that everyone has greatness inside of them. Everyone has a special talent and a special gift. How would you like your greatness to shine? Is there more for you to do to live your best life? Are you living your best life?

I recall being at a football awards banquet and I had written a poem that I wanted to share with my team. When I got ready to spring from my seat, my father grabbed me by the arm and asked, "What are you doing?" I told him I wanted to read a poem for my team. He told me, "No, don't do that! Only girls do that!" My stepmom told my dad, "It's fine, he can read the poem." But my dad strongly insisted and repeated, "No, do not read the poem." I sat back down, dejected and uninspired.

A short period later my father asked me if I thought I could be a boxer. He had been a boxer in the Army. I told my father, "I can't be a boxer. I'm a football player." My father let out this horrific, thunderous roar of a sound. "Can't? Never use that word!" he exclaimed. "Never say you can't. You can do anything you want to do as long as you pick up a book and read, then apply yourself to what you've learned and never give up!"

Talk about being a tad bit confused. One minute, my father was holding me back (by not letting me read that poem to my team); the next, he's lifting me up by telling me I can do anything. In the end, the message I believe my father was working to convey to me was: You are a leader, be aware of how and when you show your emotions, always be strong, and work to persevere over any situation. That's real talk!

And then there was my mother's influence.

My mother always wanted me to have the best education. Prior to entering high school, she suggested that I take the entry tests for two prominent college preparatory high schools. For weeks she would pester me to ask if I had taken the tests. Each time I responded that, no, I had not yet taken the tests. I have never been a good test taker. I get nervous and experience some anxiety of failing before even attempting the task of taking the test. One day my mother demanded that I take the tests immediately. I told her I would just to appease her, but the truth is I never actually took those tests.

Several weeks later she followed up once again, asking if I had received the results from the tests. Not telling the truth, I replied, "Yes, but I did not make the cut." My mother told me, "Those people don't know what they're talking about. You are an A/B student as long as you apply yourself appropriately and do your work." My mother has always believed in me even when I doubted myself.

I'm sure you've heard the old saying, "You can be anything you want to be, all you have to do is work hard at it." Well I'm not buying it, nor am I selling it. I am breaking the mold.

That old saying has become a go-to quote or a societal norm that people say to one another to inspire or encourage. Unfortunately, some societal norms are taken as truth without verifying or questioning their validity.

I am challenging you to evaluate societal norms and look beyond their face value. Truth matters more than societal norms. How do you find the truth? You dig, dig, dig to find the real truth.

Hearing that old saying over and over, year after year, prompted me to ask questions and dig, dig, dig for the answers. Yes, I received the message that I could be anything I wanted to be, but I needed concrete answers. I needed to learn *how*.

My mother Medina was always an educator—not only to her own biological children, but to children of all ages who crossed her path. It didn't matter if you were age 1 or age 100; it didn't matter. My mother encouraged people, whether loved ones or foes, to be their best. She pushed, challenged, and inspired

3

everyone to find the appropriate tools, techniques, and strategies to live their best lives.

With the inspiration of my mother and the support of my father, step mom, god parents, and a host of allies helping me work through trials and tribulations, successes and failures, growth and setbacks, research and failed experiments, I slowly began to live my best life. On my journey, I discovered four of life's most important principles that affect everyone personally and/or professionally.

You will find answers detailing how to live your best life in the CDIS model. I am going to introduce you to each principle, take you step by step through each process, and guide you through discovering or reconnecting to your "Why." Your successful journey through this book will assist you in nurturing your greatness and inspire you to be persistent, insistent and consistent in all that you do.

The CDIS principles cross cultural boundaries, help individuals cut through mediocrity, serve as a call to action, and lead to inspiring and enhancing greatness and success. Individuals are constantly searching for solutions, improvements and excellence. The CDIS model is fluid and interconnected, allowing you to take advantage of any principle or process when and where you need it most in your personal and/or professional life.

COACHING DREAMS INTO SUCCESS
High-Performance Move To Action

Balance
EVAL
Enter, Values,
Allocate, Look

Branding
SING
Strengths, Intentional Acts,
Necessary Message, Growth

WHY

Vision
DREAM
Dare, Research, Eagle
Eye, Associates, Mentor

Strategy
OGSM
Objectives, Goals,
Strategy, Measures

CDIS Principles

ARE YOU LIVING YOUR "WHY"?

Your "Why" is the core element connecting the four CDIS principles. Knowing your "Why" means simply understanding your reason, purpose, or intent, which is the energy source for *Coaching Dreams Into Success*. As you study and practice, practice, practice the CDIS model, pay close attention to the process acronyms. The acronyms are designed to assist you with remembering the process steps for each principle.

Now follow closely as I give you a brief overview of the four CDIS principles. The CDIS principles are Balance, Vision, Strategy and Branding. Prior to studying each of the (CDIS) principles, you may have found yourself in a state of flux without a prosperous solution. Never again do you have to be stuck. The CDIS principles have their own distinct and specific process that you can implement with ease. For certain you will have a solution that works. The CDIS principles and processes are fluid and interactive, meaning they can be used at any time or in any combination. The essential element that must always be prevalent is your "Why" because it connects to everything and provides the fuel to keep you going.

The first principle that I'm going to start you out with is Balance. Balance is a state of being in life. Balance paints a picture of what an individual's life looks and feels like. When you know about your Balance, your Vision becomes clearer.

Vision is highly important to living the quality of life you want for yourself. Having uncluttered dreams and hope, resulting from Balance awareness and control, will fuel your Vision. It is difficult to have clear vision, dreams or hope if your Balance is all out of whack. Dreams have power and can lead to increased energy, courage, and aspiration. Cultivating a focused dream into a laser sharp vision and from a laser sharp vision into reality requires focus, well-planned strategy and the proper alliances. As you read and work your way through the CDIS book, I anticipate you will experience some ah-ha's and discover strategies that will assist you with your Vision.

When Balance and Vision are in play, with awareness, understanding and clarity, naturally the next step is developing and implementing effective and efficient Strategy. Great Strategy is designed and implemented to provide direction on how you are going to manage the distribution and allocation of resources to ensure your goals are being met to achieve your objective.

Thinking about what you would like people to know about you and living your best life (driven by your "Why") are considerable points that speak loudly about who you are and your Brand. When you are Balanced, or know what your Balance looks like, when your Vision is laser sharp, and your Strategies are moving you to action for achievement and performance, you are going to shine. Your work and output done with consistency will build discipline. Your discipline acts as a magnetic source that will attract similar value-based people, opportunity, and abundance to you.

At this point in the CDIS process, you are cultivating and strengthening your Brand. Branding is the practice of creating a name, symbol or design that identifies and differentiates a product from other products. Your name, your work, and your results are the product. You are the Brand. Don't let anyone step up and take control of your narrative. Be assertive, intentional and persuasive with your actions that are going to influence and speak about your Brand.

In Chapter 2, you will have the opportunity to discover or reconnect with your "Why." Don't be shy.

DISCOVER YOUR "WHY"

Like many people, I have wondered, why am I on this earth? I remember wrestling with the question, what is my purpose? It began to get tougher in high school and college when I had to study psychology and read the opinions, hypotheses, and research of psychologists like Abraham Maslow, Carl Rogers, Kurt Goldstein, and others. I thought those guys were going to provide me with the answer, when in fact they confused the heck out of me! My expectation was wrong. In the end, what I received from studying those guys was the inspiration to look within, to study myself and figure out what makes me tick. Through self-reflection, I learned that I am tough, that I love to share information with people, that I enjoy connecting with people, and that I'm a good listener.

After graduating from Murray State University, I began my job hunt to start my work career. During a job interview with the Kroger Company, the interviewer asked me why I thought he should hire me. I gave him all the standard pat answers. This went on for two rounds. On the third round, I decided to give him my real "Why."

I told him I was a family man with a new family, new wife and new baby, and that I wanted to be a great father, husband, and provider for my family. I told him that as an ex-athlete with many accomplishments, I had a great work ethic, and that I planned to come to work every day and work my way up the ladder. And, I told him, if ever the job became too big for me, he would never have to terminate me because I was man enough to let him know that I couldn't handle the work. I finished by telling him that I would love to work with the Kroger Company.

The interviewer stood up, extended his hand and said, "Congratulations, Donald, you're hired. Welcome to the family." As I extended my hand to seal the deal, with just a slight smile I remember thinking to myself, "Really, that was all it took? All I had to do was summon the courage and confidence to be authentic, to tell the interviewer my 'Why'? Wow!"

That was a significant day in my life. I was at the beginning of discovering my "Why."

Your "Why" is the reason or purpose for whatever you do. Sometimes your "Why" is tough to stay connected to. There are always forces that push and pull against your "Why," making it hard to be committed, faithful, and actionable. Often the fear of being accountable rises up, or the comfort of being lazy sets in, and suddenly fulfillment is nowhere in sight. But when your "Why" is defined, clear, and never out of sight or out of touch, it is the catalyst for fulfillment, satisfaction, and a sense of achievement.

Often when I am facilitating CDIS to a class, I ask the question: How many people here know their "Why"? How many people are living their "Why"? Consistently, three-fourths of the people in the classroom respond they have yet to define their "Why" and/or are not living their "Why."

So what about you? Do you know your "Why"? Are you living your "Why"?

Following are three short stories demonstrating the power of "Why."

I once heard NBA great Kobe Bryant say that he decided he was going to get up in the morning at 4am and start his workouts because he figured the best way to get ahead of his competition was to outwork them. What was Kobe's "Why"? At the age of six years old, Kobe knew he wanted to be a basketball player and one day play professionally in the NBA. Kobe's lifetime quest has been to get the best out of himself every day. He chose basketball as his pursuit to learn discipline, to experience joy, and to release frustration. Kobe wanted to be recognized as one of the all-time great NBA players in the world. Kobe desired to surpass NBA legend Michael Jordan. So he watched videos of Michael's moves, practiced them relentlessly, and got up at 4am in the morning and outworked his competition to earn his way to basketball greatness! Kobe went on to play 20 years in the NBA, during which time he won five NBA Championships, was an 18-time All-Star, a 15-time All NBA, and a 12-time All Defense, along with a host of other accomplishments. Though Kobe's playing career has ended, he is still living his "Why" to get the best out of himself every day. I suggest you check out Kobe's "Five Pillars of the Mamba Mentality."

After several discussions about discovering your "Why" and trusting yourself, breakthroughs often occur. For example, a long-time coaching client of mine shared with me one day that he was finally going to live life through *his* lens and not through the lens of what he thought would satisfy his parents. I asked my client what prompted his new perspective.

He answered, "Two days ago, I was sitting by the lake at the park. I was thinking to myself, I am always trying to do things the way my parents tell me and suggest. I continuously work to satisfy them and live life the way I think they want me to live life. But never have they affirmed my actions or my work. Consequently, as you know, I have low self-confidence, self-esteem and self-concept. I remember it was a bright clear sunny day as I gazed into the lake with reflection and hope; it was almost as if I could see myself in the water. I asked myself the question, what do I really want during this life? With every fiber in me, I resisted the standard answer of 'to make my parents happy.' I knew immediately I had to begin to see life through a different lens. The new lens for viewing my life was reflected back to me as I looked deep into the lake. I knew at that moment that owning my own 'Why' would be my answer to living my best life."

My coaching client had several ah-ha's and decided to change his lens to how he views life.

During multiple challenging coaching engagements with a client where the goal was to increase her performance results from good to great, I began to recognize that the coaching client was being emotionally dominated by a loved one. The client found it difficult in the work setting to believe in her ideas, lacked confidence to finish projects, and was quick to go on a verbal attack. I reminded my client about many of her great successes and accomplishments. I asked my client if she was responsible for her actions and if she possessed a dream that she would like to fulfill. She indicated that she did. I asked her if she was living her "Why." She responded, "No. Maybe that's why I'm stuck."

I simply gave my client permission to unleash herself, disown the personal attacks, and take full ownership of being great, confident, and successful. She took off the veil of negative association and began to live her "Why." My client has been living an excellent life ever since. She just needed someone to believe in her more that she believed in herself.

Your "Why" is powerful! It connects to everything you do, everything you want to accomplish, and everything that you are. Your "Why" connects to your Balance, Vision, Strategy and Branding.

Here is what your "Why" will do for you:

- Your "Why" strengthens your core values
- Your "Why" is your get-back-on-track and stay-on-track tool
- Your "Why" is your fuel and your energy source for sustainability
- Your "Why" gives you the focus to sharpen your vision and discipline
- Your "Why" is the hope that keeps your dreams alive

If you are attempting to discover, enhance or improve your "Why" so you can live a more authentic life, you may find it necessary to make a change in your philosophical or motivational approach. Even if you are okay with your current approach, consider the following quote:

> ## *"If you always do what you've always done, you'll always get what you've always got."*
> — Jessie Potter, *The Milwaukee Sentinel* (1981)

Often regarded as the nation's #1 Life and Business Strategist, Tony Robbins says, "Change can happen in an instant." My experience and research have led me to believe that the reason why change can happen in an instant is because many of life's experiences have prepared us to make a conscious decision to change when the proper stimuli are present. I believe Tony Robbins was talking about connecting to your "Why."

One essential element to living a life of authenticity involves shaping your conversations and being intentional with the way you communicate with your "Why." When you communicate with your "Why" as a driving force, it will allow others to hear and feel your passion, believe your words of commitment, and trust your intent to Move To Action (MTA). Your "Why" is a powerful communication link.

> ## *"At the speed of trust comes decisions."*
> — Stephen Covey

Look at how the "Why" of a handful of well-known brands determined the messaging communicated to their customers:

BRAND	"WHY" MESSAGING
Walmart	Save money. Live better.
Disney	The Happiest Place on Earth
3M	Innovation
UPS	What Can Brown Do for You?
Nike	Just Do It

Or how about LeBron James – "Strive for Greatness," Ellen DeGeneres – "Just Keep Swimming," or Warren Buffet – "Never do anything in life if you would be ashamed of seeing it printed on the front page of your hometown newspaper for your family and friends to see." When these companies and individuals contextualize their conversation with their "Why," they connect to their audience and they are able to build relationships with their constituents in an honest, authentic way.

Do you want to see the power of your "Why"? The challenge is yours! I believe in you. Connect to your "Why" now.

Exercise 1: Take a Few Minutes to Recommit or Discover your "WHY"

Remember, everybody has something that sometimes gets in the way, something that knocks them off track, something that slows them down.

Write on a piece of paper all those things that get in your way. It doesn't matter what it is—energy robbers, haters, oxygen thieves, barriers, back stabbers, roadblocks, etc.—write them down on a single sheet of paper. Once you have compiled your list, look at it closely. Now close your eyes and imagine yourself walking to a distant place—it could be your favorite park, lake, walking trail or a place that only exists in your mind. Just pick a place where you can dispose of that list. The disposal site may be a little difficult to get to, but you can get there if you need to. Be sure that the disposal place is far enough away that if you ever need to see it again, you can. However, it should barely be in your sight.

Now, literally, ball up, tear up, and destroy the list of things that keep getting in your way. Ball up, tear up, and destroy the list that you will no longer give power to. Ball up, tear up, and destroy the list so it can no longer still your *will* or *want* so you can do whatever you set your mind to.

Never ever give power again to the inhibitors on the list you destroyed. Never let anything on that list keep you from living your "Why." Your "Why" is what drives you. When faced with difficult or challenging situations, you are going to call on your "Why." You are going to take control of living your authentic best life because your "Why" is your foundation.

Exercise 2: Go Deeper

Next, take a few minutes to think about:

- what drives you

- what motivates you to want to get up in the morning

- what makes you happy

- what inspires you to give your best

Think about when life knocks you down, what drives you to get back up? Your "Why" is your purpose. What are those things that bring you joy? What do you care about more than you care about yourself?

In the table on the following page, write your thoughts about these questions as well as the following:

- What inspires you?

- What do you love about life?

- What is the passion that you have in your heart?

- What are you most thankful for when you are alone thinking about how fortunate you are?

Discover Your...

"WHY"

> Throw away the inhibiting F.E.A.R.
> (False Evidence Appearing Real)

WRITING YOUR "WHY"

When defining your "Why" on paper, make sure it:

- reads with passion

- is clear, concise and compelling

- is written in the present tense

- sounds authentically like you

Here are a few examples of well-written "Why" statements:

"I am an awesome provider for my family that I love tremendously. I work diligently to be a subject matter expert in social media communication to help grow and improve relationships with people all around the world."

"I am building a legacy of abundance, hope and achievement."

"To live a life of simple pleasure."

Your "Why" needs to only make sense to you. You are the sole owner of your "Why." Considering the thoughts that you journaled, take a few moments to construct your "Why."

This is my... "WHY"

CHAPTER 3

BALANCE

Balance: An even or acceptable distribution of something or somethings of value that equal satisfaction.

When President Barack Obama and his family were residing in the White House, the entire family had to make a transition to a much more rigorous schedule. Time together as a family unit was important to the Obama family. Mrs. Obama knew her daughters wanted to see their Dad. She noticed how the President's schedule was affecting their two daughters going to bed at a proper time during the week in preparation for their school day. Understanding the need for more structure so there could be better balance between work and family time, the Obamas agreed on a time where the President would be home for their evening family meal at the dinner table. By prioritizing their family "Why" and taking action, the Obama family was able to restore balance in their daily lives.

In 1993, I joined a statistical group that is well-known by a huge percentage of Americans. I got divorced. Three years later, I met my current best friend and wife. I knew when I met her that if I ever wanted to have a successful relationship with another woman, I would need at least three things. First, I would have to be open to communicate about any subject at any time—especially the tough subjects, like money. Second, I would need someone who believed in my dreams and who I could share my dreams with. Third, it was important for me to be in a relationship with someone who loves family. I got all three and then some.

Fast forward to 2003, when I began my consulting company, Thoughts Developed. When I initially began as a consultant, my areas of focus were scattered across more than six disciplines and I was kind of all over the place. Someone suggested that I attend the Association for Talent Development national conference in San Diego. The conference was a true blessing for me. One of my great moments came when I had an opportunity to meet author, speaker, and business consultant Ken Blanchard and his son Scott Blanchard. The mentoring advice that they gave me was to "find one or two areas where you are proficient and master those one or two areas. Once you master the one or two areas, continue to perform your work and work to improve upon your areas of expertise every day." Ken was very gracious by posing with me in a photo for my keepsake, and I have been following his great advice ever since.

Evident by fact, I have constantly been working to have good balance in my life. I work on me consistently. I found a great partner who loves family and we communicate well together with transparency. My work is continuously evolving in leadership and communication, and I make sure to carve out time for entertainment and relaxation. Juggling these aspects of life is what I call Balance.

Unfortunately, most people find that balance is a difficult thing to achieve, particularly in the age of electronics. These are some of the comments that I often hear: "It's tough." "There's not enough time in the day." "There are a lot of forces that tug at me." "I need more help." "I need more money." "I need better direction." "I need more focus."

I am going to share with you what gave me great insight to what really affects balance. You will be able to use the CDIS Balance process strategy at any time to evaluate, reposition and cognitively manage balance in your life to achieve your expected outcomes.

There are four primary areas where we spend the majority of our awake hours. I call these the four Balance Areas, and they are: Self, Family, Work, and Social. You must give Balance significant attention because when you're out of Balance, it's sometimes tough to recognize it. In life we are pushed and pulled by many different forces that affect how we feel, what we do, and how we think. When assessing what Balance looks like and why it feels the way it feels, you must be willing to take a deep introspective view of yourself. It's not always easy or comfortable to look in the mirror and come face to face with your own truths. However, the CDIS Balance process helps to synergize the activities that affect your personal and professional Balance in life. Most often Balance is not equally distributed 25% per Balance Area. There are both fixed and variable factors that affect how much time we can devote to each. But even though Balance is often a moving target, with attention, we can create a measure of Balance stability.

If you don't have Balance, then most often you will have just the opposite: chaos! Chaos causes a lot of hectic situations, indecisions and strife. Sometimes chaos can be good. Believe it or not, sometimes chaos is planned. But whatever the situation, Balance remains the more desirable alternative.

Let's take a look at each Balance Area in more detail.

- **Self Balance** is dedicated to developing confidence, awareness, concept, esteem, spirituality, technical skills, interpersonal skills, leadership skills, subject matter acumen, cultural competence, and the like.

- **Family Balance** is dedicated to nurturing the family union, instilling and living Core Values and principles, teaching and learning how to love, and working to provide choice, comfort, peace, education and legacy.

- **Work Balance** is dedicated to generating earnings and resources that can be utilized for expenses, provide for allowances, and afford the opportunity of pleasure. Whether you're a business owner, an employee or a full-time student, this is your Work.

- **Social Balance** is dedicated to developing your tribe of networks that provide opportunities for support, fun, political gain, servant leadership, philanthropy, personal development, and the like.

Think of Balance characteristically like a lion. Lions are strong, disciplined, focused, and strategic. They are very family oriented, protective, and social. Lions also have clear roles and responsibilities connected to strong values.

THE CONNECTION BETWEEN BALANCE AND VALUES

Values play a huge role in Balance. Sometimes Values and Principles are used interchangeably. For the sake of comparison, I offer that Values are emotional. They can guide how we feel, what we think, and determine what is important. Principles are behavioral. Principles guide by standards, rule, protocol, policy and procedure. Principles lead to how we are going to act. Values determine if we are going to act. Values are those things that we hold near and dear to our hearts. Often our values will not be compromised.

Values drive behaviors. What we value will get attention and what we give attention to is what we will act upon. Be certain to commit to memory the phrase, "values drive behaviors." This phrase will help you to eliminate costly decisions and encourage you to choose well-thought-out strategic alternatives.

Coming up are the process steps for Balance. You will have the opportunity to discover how important it is to always be conscious of your time, priorities and values. Your input in this process is going to give you an image of what your current level of Balance looks like. If you're like most people, once you've established your current level of Balance, you'll need to ask yourself some tough questions if you want to improve, grow and/or change.

What's really beautiful is that after people ask themselves the tough questions about Balance, they're able to use the other principles of Vision, Strategy, and Branding with their processes to generate additional solutions. So let's get started with the Balance process.

PRINCIPLE: BALANCE

E nter	Determine your Awake Hours by subtracting your sleep hours from the total hours in a day.
V alues	
A llocate	
L ook	

Awake Hours are the hours in each day that you have available to spend in each Balance Area. Whatever your Awake Hours are, often it seems like there just aren't enough hours in a day to do all that needs to be accomplished. Time management is a serious issue for many people. If you could manage time better, it would be like waving a magic wand. But there is no magic wand. There are only those things that you need to get done during your Awake Hours.

Do the simple math to determine your Awake Hours (AH). Subtract your sleep hours from the total hours in one day (for example, 24 − 6 = 18 AHs). If you'd prefer to do this exercise based on a longer time period—weekly, bi-weekly or monthly

—that's fine. The process is the exactly the same. Now that you have your AH, write them in the center of the target below.

Hit the target with your Awake Hours

On our journey toward better Balance, we need to learn how to compartmentalize and prioritize our Awake Hours using Core Values as filters. We'll explore that in the next section.

PRINCIPLE: BALANCE

E nter	Determine your Awake Hours by subtracting your sleep hours from the total hours in a day.
V alues	Determine your three to five Core Values for each Balance Area: Self, Family, Work and Social.
A llocate	
L ook	

When you think of the things that are important to you, naturally some things will rank higher in importance than others. Often the scale of importance will range from little to no value, up to extremely high value. What you determine you are going to act upon will be based on the scale of importance that you've assigned to something or someone. Synthesizing the importance of those rankings is how you will ultimately determine your Values.

As a complex human being who lives a very dynamic and fluid life, you have a multitude of values that shape your paradigm of decision making. Think about the Core Values you have, all the things you say that are important to you. Think about your values that drive how you make decisions, and your values that energize how you move about your day in the Balance Areas.

In the chart on the following page (or on a separate sheet of paper), list as many of your values as you can for each BA. Initially you should have a minimum range of 10-15 values per BA. It does not matter if the values duplicate from one BA to another BA.

Take your time; don't rush to be finished after writing your first thoughts. Think deeper about what else is important to you. If you get stuck, don't worry. Just refer back to your "Why." Ask yourself questions that provoke the reason you determined your "Why" to be what you defined it.

Build your list to be huge! This is critically one of the most important steps in the process. Take your time.

Write all your Values in the BA sections on the following page. Remember, it's okay if your Values duplicate from one BA to another BA. Build a big list of 10 or more Values per section.

An example of values: *trust, fun, money, family, timeliness, work, transparency, education, teamwork, etc.* Remember, Values drive behaviors.

VALUES

FAMILY	WORK
SELF	SOCIAL

Chart 1

I remember delivering a leadership course to a group of directors for an organization. One of the organization's core values was employee development. Okay, we're on the same page … or so I thought. I asked the directors, all of whom had staff responsibility, "How many of you are developing staff for leadership roles and responsibility to one day have someone succeed you?" No one raised their hand. So I thought to myself maybe I needed to rephrase the question. I tried again. "How many of you realize the importance of human capital succession planning, and do you have someone that you are grooming to sit in your position one day?" Once again, no one raised their hand.

I immediately put on my jacket, gathered my belongings, and headed toward the door. Someone shouted, "Mr. White, where are you going?" I responded, "It has become apparent to me that we have different values. Pursuant to the questions that I asked, there was no response acknowledging the need for growth and development of staff. I know that if we do not have similar to the same values, we are going to have conflict. This is not a good start."

The class of directors asked if I would come back and give them another opportunity. I obliged. We discussed values and the importance of employee development. We also established a working understanding of leadership versus bossing. Then we proceeded with our work and had a productive session.

Values drive behaviors! What we value will get attention, what gets attention can be measured, and what gets measured can get done. Check your values list. Be sure that you have listed all of the great and important values that move you to action.

PRINCIPLE: BALANCE

E nter	Determine your Awake Hours by subtracting your sleep hours from the total hours in a day.
V alues	Determine your three to five Core Values for each Balance Area: Self, Family, Work and Social.
A llocate	Plot the time/percentage of your Awake Hours in each Balance Area on a pie chart.
L ook	

Congratulations, nice work on developing your big list of values! It's nice to know that we are on the same page in the belief that Values drive behaviors, right? Now, I want you to think about how you move about your day during your Awake Hours based on the list of values you determined that are important to you. To understand Balance, it is important to give attention to how you move about the day during your Awake Hours. Based on the list of values that you generated for each BA, ask yourself the following questions:

- Are you accomplishing what you set out to do?

- Are you maximizing your efforts? If not, Why?

- Are you putting off for tomorrow what you can do today?

- Are you making excuses versus being accountable?

- Do you think your decisions and actions are sometimes clouded by the long list of values that you generated?

If you answered yes to any of the questions above, then you are going to love the results of the forthcoming process step. This is where you help yourself to become more productive, profitable, effective and efficient.

Go back and review your list of values for each BA. You should notice that some of the values are very similar to each other. Your values function like the lens of a camera; they can be telescopic, focusing inward or outward. The sharper you can focus the lens of the camera, the better picture you will have. Likewise, the sharper you can focus your values, the better decisions you will make, and the more efficient and effective you will be.

Go back to your values and pair them down to get three to five Core Values (CV) for each BA. CVs are your most important extremely high-ranking Values. Your Core Values will seldom change (if ever) and you will usually act upon them with certainty throughout your life. No doubt, there is one thing for certain, and two things are for sure. Values drive behaviors. What you value will get attention, and what you give attention to is what you will act upon.

For clarity and sharpness, transfer your three to five pared-down CVs for each BA to the table below or a separate sheet of paper.

CORE VALUES

FAMILY	WORK
SELF	SOCIAL

Chart 2

As we discussed earlier, lack of time management is too often the enemy of Balance. Can you manage time? Ponder these two words, *manage* and *time*. The word *manage* has a variety of definitions including to handle or direct with a degree of skill, and to control or organize someone or something. A definition for *time* is the indefinite continued progress of existence and events in the past, present, and future. Nowhere in all my research have I ever found evidence that would lead me to believe that anyone can manage time. Based on the definitions, in my opinion, the idea of time management is a fallacy. Time management is another societal norm that I challenge you not to take as a truth.

Often organizations spend large sums of money providing courses to their employees on time management in hopes that the staff will grow to become more efficient, effective and productive. But there's a different way to frame time management. I call it Compartmentalized Priorities in Time or CPT.

My view is that you have no control over time. However, you can use time as a measurement. In order to measure anything, you must have a beginning and an end. With time, you always have a beginning and an end. Instead of trying to manage time, focus on managing things you truly can control, like tasks, money, business, files, processes, and the like. Time allows you to consciously and strategically evaluate your actions and your progress toward whatever your objective might be. That's right. Once again, it has come back around to "Values drive behaviors," especially as it relates to time.

Pay particularly close attention to this: **Your Core Values drive your behaviors during your Awake Hours.** The sum of what you accomplish is based on your CV plus what you do during your Awake Hours.

Equation: CV+AH = Balance

To determine your particular "Balance" sum, use the following process steps:

Think about your Core Values and how they affect your actions during a normal day. Based on your thoughts, generally how many hours do you spend in each BA (Self, Family, Work, Social)? Write those hours in the table on the next page.

Next, look back on the target page and get your AH.

Now determine the percentage of time for each BA. Divide your BA hours by your AHs and write the percentage in the table on the next page.

Example: Self; 3 BA/hrs. ÷ 16 AHs = 18.75٪

Repetition is the mother of all learning. Once again, record your CV in the table on the following page.

CALCULATE YOUR "BALANCE" SUM

FAMILY	WORK
Hrs. %	Hrs. %
SELF	SOCIAL
Hrs. %	Hrs. %

Chart 3

"And now for the rest of the story," as a veteran news man named Paul Harvey used to say.

In the circle below, plot the lines in the pie chart that represent your BA percentage of time. List the BA, hours, and percentage of time in the proportioned areas appropriately. Voila! Allakazam! You just created a data-driven image based on your input of what your personal and professional Balance looks like. Based upon your Core Values, your Awake Hours, and what you prioritize to do during your Awake Hours, you now have a visual image of what your Balance looks like.

Fact: You cannot manage time; you can only manage those things that you do within the time and space you have. Fact: You can compartmentalize and prioritize what needs to get attention and executed with action within a timeframe.

Balance Wheel

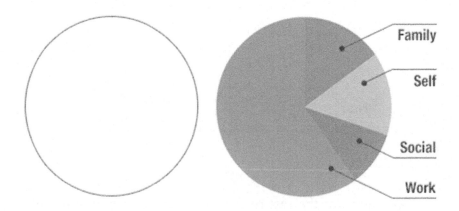

Chart 4: What are your tough questions?

PRINCIPLE: BALANCE

E nter	Determine your Awake Hours by subtracting your sleep hours from the total hours in a day.
V alues	Determine your three to five Core Values for each Balance Area: Self, Family, Work and Social.
A llocate	Plot the time/percentage of your Awake Hours in each Balance Area on a pie chart.
L ook	Assess the picture of your Balance and ask yourself the tough question for growth and improvement.

You may recall a few pages back when I said that at some point, you would have to ask yourself some tough questions. Well, now is that time! This part can be challenging, but it's necessary. This is where the rubber meets the road. This is where the light switch is either on or off. This is where if you fall, do you make the decision to get back up? This is where you determine whether good is going to be the enemy to great.

Look at your CV, time and percentage of time for each BA in your Balance Wheel and ask yourself the following questions:

- What is it that I might be missing?
- So what?
- Now what?
- Then what?
- What's next?

Analyze the big picture. Begin to strategize by creating the Vision you want to see, constructing and planning the Strategies and Goals you want to accomplish, and committing yourself to living your best life and developing your Brand to be awesome in all that you do and represent.

Leverage your knowledge, wisdom, and experience for your continued growth by associating with mentors and/or coaches. Read often and share in an exchange of knowledge with people who have similar values as yours. Another person whom you may choose to associate with does not have to share the exact same values as yours; just make sure they are similar. And if you associate with someone who has totally dissimilar values than yours, be sure to recognize such attributes based on your Core Values and move away from them decisively at the appropriate time. Your gut instinct will likely never misguide you. As I like to say:

> *"If you can't **change** the people around you, then change the **people** around you."*
> — Coach Don White

The fact that you now have a grasp of what your Balance looks and feels like means you are in a better position than before to see what's in front of you, down the road, and around the corner. Your balance gives you clearer vision for your pursuits, no matter how big or small, personal or professional. The clearer your vision, the more directed and focused you will be in moving to action with deliberate intention. This is a perfect time for me to introduce the second CDIS principle, Vision, and its process.

CHAPTER 4

VISION

Vision: A vivid image and/or idea that is so clear, its distinction is unmistakable, inspirational and undeniable.

Apple Computer Company was co-founded in 1976 by Steve Wozniak, Ronald Wayne, and Steve Jobs. Steve Jobs was the guiding force for the marketing and innovation direction of anything and everything Apple. During his first stint with Apple, Jobs had a vision for the world where everyone had a personal computer (PC). That vision drove the company to a level of success that exceeded everyone's expectation. Over time, however, a power struggle ensued between Jobs and then-CEO John Sculley, leading the board of directors to eventually fire Jobs. Jobs left Apple and started Pixar with some success. But after 10 years apart, with Apple losing its sense of direction and pioneering spirit, Jobs and Apple would reunite. Jobs didn't just return to run a company. In his words, his return was, "to make

a contribution to the world by making tools for the mind that advance humankind." One of Jobs' vision mantras was, "Be Different."

Think of Vision characteristically like an Eagle. The Eagle is brave, bold, daring and audacious. It has extremely great vision and focus. It soars fearlessly with passion, pragmatism, perspective, personality, and perseverance.

If not tended to with the greatest care in the world, your vision can be blurry, unfocused, misdirected, without definition, or even blacked-out due to improper lighting. With poor Vision comes less than optimal achievement.

During my more than 30 years of facilitating conversations about Vision, I've noticed that people tend to guard their visions closely. Generally, people are guarded about sharing their Visions because they have been taken advantage of one too many times, or they are simply tired of people dousing their dreams. Today you get to take full control of developing your dreams into your Vision, and with growing confidence, I predict that you will connect with the right people to help bring your vision into reality. I want you to know that I am here to support you. What you are going to experience in this CDIS Vision process will be a game changer as long as you are willing to play the game at a high level and follow the process.

Are you a person who holds your vision close to your heart, locked and stored in your brain, journalized and safely secured under a password, and safely locked away? If so, don't think you are by yourself! Most certainly you are not.

Vision is very powerful, exciting, energizing and restorative. Consider the following, some of my favorite quotes on Vision:

- *"Where there is no Vision, the people will perish."* (Proverbs 29:18)

- *"If you don't have a vision, you're going to be stuck in what you know. And the only thing you know is what you've already seen."* (Iyanla Vanzant)

- *"One's vision is not a road map but a compass."* (Peter Block)

- *"If you are working on something that you deeply care about, you don't have to be pushed. The vision will pull you."* (Steve Jobs)

- *"Champions aren't made in the gyms. Champions are made from something they have inside them—a desire, a dream, a vision."* (Muhammad Ali)

Imagine a five-year-old boy jumping up and down on his mom's bed. His mom asks him what he wants to be when he grows up. The young boy, full of excitement and energy, replies, "I want to be a preacher, Mom!" The boy carries this vision of being a preacher in his mind his entire life. Often during the journey of the boy's life—in school, in groups and on teams—he was called upon to be the spokesperson. On one occasion, as a senior in high school, the school principal selects the boy to be a spokesperson alongside the student body president and vice-president for a television program highlighting area high schools. On the opposite end of the spectrum, the boy is also told on numerous occasions that he should not even think about speaking in public forums. As the boy continues his journey through life, he is conflicted about seeking opportunities to live his dream.

Sometimes his confidence is shaken, but he keeps his boyhood dream in his mind. One day the boy, who is now a man, meets this lady who believes in his vision. This lady not only believes in his vision, she cultivates an opportunity for him to showcase his gift and bring his dream into a vision and his vision into reality. Today, I am that boy who has grown into a man, Coach Don White. My dream was always inside of me. I could always see my dream, and the lady who believed in me and listened to my dreams ... well, she agreed that we have similar to the same values and said yes to marrying me.

I have witnessed the power of Vision on many occasions. An instance that remains very clear in my mind is when a female class participant was recording a CDIS presentation that I was delivering and wanted me to stop in the middle of the presentation. The lady raised her hand to ask a question: "Coach Don, will you hold that point for a moment while I flip my cassette?" To my dismay, this lady was serious! She flipped her cassette and I continued with my presentation. During a 15-minute break, she approached me and asked if I had a few minutes to speak with her. Eager to listen, I obliged her with the requested time. She said, "Coach Don, I would like to share my Vision with you and get your opinion to see if I am on the right track."

She told me her vision was to start a non-profit organization for the purpose of taking high school seniors on college tours, and she also planned to open a group home for young girls. She also asked if I would pay a visit to her job and look at her vision board. I agreed. At the time, she was a counselor at an elementary school. When I arrived, she escorted me to her office. Front and center, the first item I saw in her office was her vision board. Her vision board was right on track. She had cut out pictures, phrases and words that represented the direction she was strategizing and the outcomes she desired and expected. We had a brief discussion and I made a few coaching points. The lady is extremely successful today. Her non-profit organization is called Step Higher. They conduct sold-out college tours every year. She also opened her group home called Nella's.

On another occasion, the University of Cincinnati Facilities Management division wanted to spice up their professional development program for their front-line staff. They had a two-pronged vision: (1) increase the professional development class participation for front-line employees; and (2) increase employee enrollment into the University accredited colleges.

I was contracted to work with the University to bring their vision into reality. Conducting a cultural scan to determine the interest of the front-line employees gave me a great platform to design and develop content that was contextual, compelling, and current. Accompanying the front-line curriculum was an eight-week leadership certificate program that I designed and delivered for first- and second-line supervisors.

The successes were fantastic. University enrollment increased, people were promoted, supervisors gained greater insight on leading versus bossing, and many people had personal breakthroughs.

Here are two of my favorite UC vision stories:

MARY'S STORY

There was a lady named Mary who attended my classes regularly. She even came to a few classes repeatedly. Strangely,

Mary never uttered a word in class. One day we had a smaller than normal class of eight people. I recognized that Mary was one of the eight people and that this was a class she had already attended previously. I asked Mary to share with the class her thoughts on having a vision and believing in your dreams.

As Mary began to speak, she told her fellow participants that she had been coming to the classes because one day she heard me talk about believing in your dreams and how to sharpen your vision. Mary said, she posed two questions to herself: "If not now, then when?" and "Why not me?" Mary went on to tell the class that she began to dream again as she followed the DREAM process, and that coming to the classes kept her inspired.

So I asked Mary, "What is your dream? What is your vision?" Mary said that she had always lived in an apartment, both as a child and as an adult. Mary said that nobody in her immediately family had ever lived in a house. Mary went on to say that she had always fantasized about living in a house where she could raise her three daughters and call it their home. I still get chills every time I tell this story.

Mary pulled out a picture that she drew of a house with a fence, flowers, grass and four windows. Each window represented a bedroom—one for each one of her daughters and one for herself. Mary completed her story by sharing that she was due to close on the purchase of her new home the next day and move into her new home the following week. Wow!

UC LEADERSHIP TEAM

During a focus group meeting with the UC leadership team, I asked the attendees if they were preparing someone to fill their role one day. No one answered me. So after a few rounds of poking and prodding with my most authoritative and commanding voice, I asked, "WHY IS NO ONE ANSWERING?" Everyone either looked at each other or down at the table, refusing to answer and be accountable. Then a brave sole lamented, "If we train people, they might see our weaknesses, vulnerabilities or faults." The gentleman explained that that type of exposure would make it harder for the supervisor to boss their people. Believe it or not, others abruptly agreed. After admonishing the group for their lack of confidence, trust and clear communication, we discussed the power of vision and how vision is better focused when you know your balance, when you are driven by values, when roles and responsibilities are clear, and when you have great strategy.

I instructed the supervisors to draw a work-related picture of something inspirational to them and then capture their picture in words. Afterwards I instructed each person to pass their picture to the person on their right. Everyone had to read and describe the other person's picture. Finally, I put them into small groups where they discussed commonalities, communication gaps, and trust.

This exercise demonstrated to the supervisors that in order to bring their vision into reality, they would have to change their approach from bossing to leading. And in order for them to lead, the supervisors began to understand they would need to share their vision consistently and be more inclusive with their staff. Many of the supervisors began to see the light and pledged to work more from the premise of leading people and managing business versus bossing people and being myopic for self only.

IMPORTANCE OF VISION

The importance of vision cannot be overstated. When you include other people in the process of developing and nurturing your vision, it is important that you surround yourself with dream makers who will encourage you to dream big, bold, daring and audacious dreams. To ensure that your dream energy is focused in the right direction, you will need to research and unearth the facts, data and statistics that support your endeavors.

You must commit action to execute your due diligence. Do not accept what appears on the surface. Get the Eagle Eye by sharpening your vision through visualization, meditation, prayer, and faith. Remember to be conscious about who you associate with. Make sure you align yourself with strategic, value-based partnerships and/or collaborations. And, of course, you want to grow progressively, so be sure to get a mentor and provide mentoring for others as well.

The bottom line is for you to use your imagination to create a happy, satisfying, beautiful, encouraging, or spiritual ideal image. Call it your dream and sharpen it into laser vision so you are directed and inspired to live your best life. Now, check out the Vision process steps and go put in the work.

PRINCIPLE: VISION

D are	Dare to Dream! Dare to believe in what you imagine. Be Big, Bold, Audacious and Unstoppable.
R esearch	
E agle Eye	
A ssociates	
M entor	

Your mind is the most powerful asset that you possess. Once you create your dreams, you have the power of choice. You have a choice to choose a strategy for bringing the dream in your mind into reality. And then you have the choice to do the work. The dreams that you create in your mind are shaped my many variables: your knowledge, wisdom, experience, explorations, storytelling, music, and/or an inner voice. If you want to create your dream and then nurture it into your vision and manifest your vision into reality, read your "Why," trust your intuition, and let your imagination flow freely. Have Fun! Let Loose! Own Your Power to Dream!

On a piece of paper or in the space provided below, take your time to draw a picture to represent the dream(s) that you dare to dream big, bold, daring and audaciously about.

YOUR DREAM SPACE

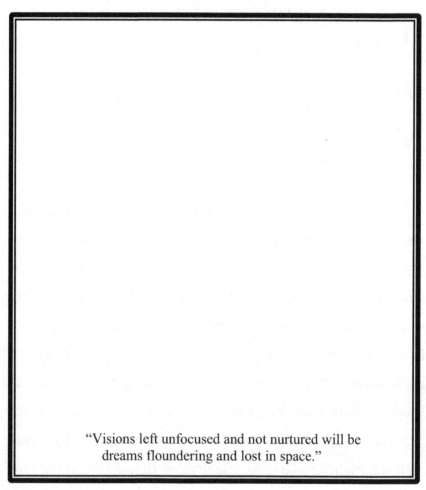

"Visions left unfocused and not nurtured will be dreams floundering and lost in space."

Chart 5

PRINCIPLE: VISION

D are	Dare to Dream! Dare to believe in what you imagine. Be Big, Bold, Audacious and Unstoppable.	
R esearch	Dig to unearth the facts, data and statistics that support your endeavors.	
E agle Eye		
A ssociates		
M entor		

Once you have decided on a dream to pursue, you must investigate. I call it Dig, Dig, Dig! It is important to be informed, prepared and knowledgeable about your dream to ensure that you are on the right track and can easily determine where your dream and passion intersects with your "Why."

I can remember National Geographic photographer Dewitt Jones explaining that he had researched about taking a journey to find a particular waterfall located deep in the jungle. The problem was it was extremely tough to access because the density of the jungle made it impossible to get there by vehicle, and not many people had successfully made the trek on foot. Dewitt had heard many accounts about the magnificent majestic waterfall. The more stories Dewitt heard about the beautiful waterfall, the more he desired to find and see it with his own eyes, as well as through the lens of his camera.

Dewitt prepared himself to enter the jungle to find the waterfall. After a long tough trek, Dewitt finally spied the waterfall he was looking for off in the distance. So what does Dewitt do next? Well, of course, he took the picture; after all, that is why he went there. He then looked at the screen of his camera to view the image. The waterfall was spectacular. But Dewitt wondered to himself, "If I could get closer, what would the shot of the waterfall look like?"

Dewitt could have settled for the surface, but he chose to Dig, Dig, Dig! He forged on, navigating his way deeper through the jungle to get closer to the waterfall. Finally, he came to another area where he could snap another picture of the waterfall. When Dewitt looked at the first picture compared to the second picture, he noticed that in the first picture there were a few tall trees in the frame of the waterfall. The second picture had no obstructions—only that spectacular waterfall, with the water free-falling from the top to the bottom and then flowing into a smaller body of water. The second waterfall picture was as beautiful and magnificent as Dewitt had ever imagined.

Source: Pixabay (Simon Bardet)

It is extremely important to research your dream so you can prepare yourself for the amount of work required to crystalize your dream into your vision. Once your dream is crystalized into your vision, your critical thinking will become keener, to where you will be able to see and uncover additional options, methods and resources. Most people begin their research online, using search engines, data mining, artificial intelligence, and discussion groups. You might also extend your internet research to government sites, discussion boards and blogs. Your public library and the Library of Congress are great sources of information as well. And joining trade associations and social organizations, volunteering, attending conferences or working a part-time job all provide fantastic platforms to conduct research.

The next couple of pages will provide you with some helpful research strategies and exercises. Following is a guideline to narrow your research efforts.

PICKING A TOPIC

1. I am researching ... (topic)
2. Because I want to find out ... (issue / question)
3. In order to ... (application – so what? / project / audience / purpose driven)

GETTING THE BEST INFORMATION

1. What are the important factors?
2. What research methodology will I use?
3. What are some benefits I will gain by doing my due diligence?

Following are some guidelines to narrow your topic research efforts. These are strategies to generate focused research questions: The table below illustrates how to pare down a broad topic to a more focused question. Follow the examples given, then use the blank columns to develop your own questions.

1. What are the main concepts of this topic?

2. What are the issues surrounding this topic?

3. What are some key terms that are being used to describe the topic?

BROAD TOPIC	RESTRICTED TOPIC	NARROWED TOPIC	RESEARCH QUESTION
Start a Business	Consulting	Growing technology in Renewable Energy	What industry is going to have the long-term highest demand?
Travel	Vacation	International locations by air and cruise line	What are the legal requirements? What is the quality and availability of health care?

Chart 6

Here's another exercise to help you generate additional focused research questions. The table below illustrates three common types of research questions. Follow the examples given and use the blank columns to develop your own questions.

Descriptive	Observational	Cause and Effect
To describe what is going on, what currently exists	Involves the direct observation of phenomena in their natural state	The reasons for and/or the consequences of an action, event, or decision
What are the three most important points of experience for a Renewable Energy consultant?	What are the real benefits of renewable energy to the lay person?	How can I ensure that my entry into the market will make an immediate impact?
What have other air and cruise line international travelers experienced?	Which air and cruise line provides the highest quality of service and amenities?	How can my out-of-pocket costs be reduced if I choose to use only a few service providers?

Chart 7

PRINCIPLE: VISION

D are	Dare to Dream! Dare to believe in what you imagine. Be Big, Bold, Audacious and Unstoppable.
R esearch	Dig to unearth the facts, data and statistics that support your endeavors.
E agle Eye	Sharpen your vision through Visualization, Meditation, Prayer and Faith.
A ssociates	
M entor	

As you work to sharpen the focus of your dream into a laser sharp vision and then bring that vision into reality, there will be many obstructions that work hard to distract you, derail you, and throw you off course. With the Eagle Eye, you will begin to see more personal growth where your "Why" becomes more resilient, your Core Values are reinforced, and the way in which you make decisions to take action is more consistent. Consistency is what helps to form what I call the "Big D" word: DISCIPLINE.

The Eagle Eye process step is going to require Faith, Prayer, Visualization and Meditation. Let's take a look at Faith and Prayer first. Faith is the evidence of things hoped for, but not yet seen. Prayer is the action of submitting oneself to an external source or higher supreme being for a variety of different reasons. Both Faith and Prayer start in the mind and they are powerful sources that energize and focus direction, decisions, and actions.

Visualization and Meditation are practices that have been used for centuries, which is not surprising given what visual people we are. Repeatedly, by way of my research over decades, I have learned that a whopping 65 percent of people learn best through visual style or a combination that includes auditory and kinesthetic. So, how can you benefit from visualization and meditation practice?

One of the most inspiring and powerful accomplishments you can experience in life is to visualize what it is that you want to manifest, and then make it happen. The power of the mind is astonishing, and when coupled with mindfulness-based practices like meditation and visualization, you can increase your ability by leaps and bounds toward creating the life that you truly desire. Meditation is simply the practice of being still and/or moving with controlled body movements, paying attention to the body, and focusing on breathing. Visualization is simply the practice of envisioning how you will react to certain experiences or what outcomes you want from your endeavors.

When I was a college sophomore student athlete playing football, my coach suggested that I should lift weights more often. I responded by writing on coach's chalkboard, "I do not lift weights." Boy, was I a stubborn guy! To the coach's credit, he said, "Donald, just give it a try. If you don't like it, don't continue to lift the weights." As long as the coach was not telling me what to do, I was okay with trying his suggestion.

Giving all the credit to my coach, during that spring of 1979, I began to lift weights with greater frequency, diligence and purpose. I got bigger, stronger and faster. So when the summer of 1979 came around and I went home, I continued my routine. I had begun to visualize that I would be this super-human athlete and that no one would be able to stop me. No one! I was so dedicated, focused and driven that I let nothing stand in the way of my weightlifting routine. My vision of being Superman became crystal clear. I only went out with my friends one night to party that summer. When I returned to school in the fall, everything was perfect. My visualization, focus, and consistent work ethic paid off. My grades improved, I made All-OVC and All Tri-State, and we won the OVC Championship. That experience gave me confidence to singularly focus in on a desired outcome. Thanks, Coach Sullivan.

I have yet to become an expert on visualization or meditation, but I am a practicing student. Many times, I have experienced great benefits from my practice. As a matter of fact, this book is a manifestation of my meditation, visualization, prayer and faith. For me, the book journey started in the fall of 2005. I was a presenter at a national conference in Florida. I thought it would be good to have a product I could sell to recoup some of my travel costs. Consequently, I wrote a short handbook, made 100 copies, and sold out. Although I sold every copy, I knew that I could produce a much better product.

With that previous success on my side, I was inspired to write a second book, but the fire and desire to write dwindled down to a flicker quickly. On several occasions I attempted to write, but I could not find the focus required to complete a good book.

Fast forward to the beginning of the year 2018. I began implementing meditation, visualization, prayer and faith every day to grow CDIS. A transformation occurred that year, and I began to write *The 4 Principles of Coaching Dreams Into Success*. Within four months, I had finished writing my manuscript.

It is my testimony that visualization and meditation work. There are as many ways to meditate and visualize as there are people who practice the disciplines. Think about star soccer player Carli Lloyd, actor Jim Carrey, media mogul Oprah Winfrey, and award-winning TV and movie star Will Smith. What do you think they all have in common? Well, the commonality between these successful people has many names.

Some people call it "the power of positive thinking." Other people like to say these people have an incredible sense of focus, or that they pray to get the results they expect. Whatever the reason, these people and thousands of other people like them who seem superhuman in their achievements, they are still like all of us in many ways. The difference is they regularly and consistently practice meditation and visualization. They are so consistent, it has become a disciplined behavior in their lives. Remember the "Big D" word: DISCIPLINE. I define Discipline as performing an act consistently that repeatedly produces the favorable outcome you expect.

I am encouraging you to explore Eagle Eye strategies more in depth. As you continue reading, you are going to be introduced to visualization and meditation strategies that are geared to sharpen your Eagle Eye. When you get comfortable with a strategy, practice that strategy consistently to build your Discipline. If you are currently practicing visualization and/or meditation, I suggest that you give additional attention to ensuring your visualization and meditation practices are connected to your "Why."

LEARNING NUGGETS

You can start your visualizing/meditation practice in a variety of ways. For example, you might:

- construct a vision board made of clippings from magazines and newspapers

- meditate in a quiet, comfortable space

- practice yoga or martial arts

- draw what you imagine on paper

- journalize your thoughts in a diary

- post images that mirror your vision in areas of your home or office where you will see them daily

Visualization Exercise #1: Image Projection

1. Identify something that you wish to accomplish, enhance or improve. This is your focal point.

2. Draw the image pictured in your mind on a separate piece of paper.

3. Place the image you drew on a surface in front of you and then place the image in your mind.

4. Close your eyes and begin to visualize in your mind the image you drew.

5. Once you visualize your image clearly, begin to include the process steps that are required for you to accomplish your endeavors. (Note: This exercise could take several attempts.)

Journal your thoughts, discoveries, or insights…

Visualization Exercise #2: Start with the End in Mind

1. Picture the perfect YOU in one, two, or three years. What does that picture look like?

2. Verbalize and describe what your picture looks like by making notes on a piece of paper.

3. Close your eyes and visualize the picture of what the perfect YOU looks like. Also, visualize one specific Move To Action (MTA) behavior that will help bring your visualization into reality.

Describe what your picture looks like…

Visualization Exercise #3: 30-Day Challenge

1. For the next 30 days, when you awake and get out of bed, think of one Big, Bold, Daring, Audacious dream you want to accomplish.

2. Envision up to three milestone steps that you are going to take to bring your vision into reality.

3. Subconsciously repeat the following statement for 2-3 minutes: "I commit to Move To Action on [name the desired accomplishment and the milestone steps]."

Example: "I commit to making 20 phone calls per day to get in front of people and know my script, so I can sell 100,000 books by February 2005."

What is your Good Morning Meditation?

_____

_____

_____

_____

_____

_____

_____

_____

_____

_____

Journal your thoughts, discoveries, or insights…

_____

_____

_____

_____

_____

_____

_____

_____

_____

_____

_____

_____

_____

Meditation Exercise #1: 4 – 7 – 8 Breathing

1. Sit or lie down and relax yourself by taking 4 deep breaths, exhaling slowly on each breath.

2. Close your eyes preferably. (You can leave them open if you wish or need to.)

3. Inhale through your nose while slowly counting to 4 in your mind (1,2,3,4).

4. Hold your breath while counting to 7 in your mind (1,2,3,4,5,6,7).

5. Exhale through your mouth while counting to 8 in your mind (1,2,3,4,5,6,7,8).

6. Do this for a minimum of 3 rounds.

Journal your thoughts, discoveries, or insights...

_____

_____

_____

_____

_____

_____

_____

_____

_____

_____

_____

_____

_____

_____

_____

_____

_____

_____

_____

_____

_____

Meditation Exercise #2: Body Scan

- Sit or lie down and relax yourself by taking 4 deep breaths, exhaling slowly on each breath.

- Close your eyes preferably. (You can leave them open if you wish or need to.)

- Start by focusing on your feet, then slowly pull your toes toward your head (breathe slowly).

- Tighten your calf muscles (breathe slowly).

- Tighten your thigh muscles (breathe slowly).

- Tighten your buttocks (breathe slowly).

- Drop your stomach to touch your spine (breathe slowly).

- Roll your shoulders backwards (breathe slowly).

- Tighten your hands into a fist (breathe slowly).

- Tighten your face muscles (breathe slowly).

- Starting from the face and working your way back down to your feet, relax each body part slowly while continuing to breathe slowly.

- Repeat this process five times.

Journal your thoughts, discoveries, or insights…

Meditation Exercise #3: Quiet Space

- Find a quiet space where you won't be interrupted.

- Sit on the floor or on a chair in an upright, erect position.

- Relax yourself by taking 4 deep breaths, exhaling slowly on each breath.

- Close your eyes.

- Relax your body and let it go limp.

- Release your mind of all thoughts.

- Breathe in through your nose slowly, and exhale through your mouth.

- Build up your focus and concentration to the point where you can do this meditation exercise for 15 – 30 minutes per sitting.

Journal your thoughts, discoveries, or insights…

PRINCIPLE: VISION

D are	Dare to Dream! Dare to believe in what you imagine. Be Big, Bold, Audacious and Unstoppable.
R esearch	Dig to unearth the facts, data and statistics that support your endeavors.
E agle Eye	Sharpen your vision through Visualization, Meditation, Prayer and Faith.
A ssociates	Align yourself strategically with value-based Partnerships and Collaborations.
M entor	

Who you associate with and *how* you associate with people can have an impressionable impact and effect on you. People typically interface with each other through Partnership and Collaboration. Partnering means to invest with shared interest in the cost and return on investment for something of mutual interest and value. Collaborating means to willingly work jointly on an event or project to complete or create something. Collaboration can be tricky and sometimes even dangerous. However, it can also be productive and profitable.

Remember earlier in the Balance section when you completed the values exercise? That's where you developed your Core Values. Remember, everything is connected to your

"Why." Who you associate with connects to your "Why" and is driven by your Core Values. Values drive behaviors. What you value will drive the actions and behaviors that you exhibit. If you subscribe to this philosophy, then surely you know that to collaborate with someone who has vastly different values than your own will not be a good idea. If you choose to collaborate with someone who has totally dissimilar values to your own, negative conflict and a waste of time will most likely be the result. It is important when collaborating or partnering to identify in the other individual similar like-minded values that will guide your decisions and actions.

A couple of years ago, one of my previous business associates informed me about a request for proposal (RFP) information meeting that he thought we should attend. I took a look at the RFP and determined that going to the meeting would be worthwhile.

After listening to the presentation and listening to how the organization answered questions, I felt very uneasy about pursuing an opportunity to earn the company's business. When my associate and I got back in the car, I could see the beam of excitement glowing across his face. I asked him his thoughts on the meeting. He responded that he felt the meeting was excellent, and that the financial opportunity was right on time. To which I responded, "Not all money is good money!"

The organization had totally different operating values than what I had. When the organization's representative began to speak about the vision and mission of the organization, it was different than what was written in the RFP. I shared with my business associate that when your values are dissimilar and you don't have alignment with your vision and mission, then chaos and strife are bound to happen. It is not a matter of *if* the chaos is going to happen, it's just a matter of *when* and at what cost.

Here's another example involving another one of my business associates. I came to know Mike through a business conference we both attended. After a few phone calls and a business lunch, Mike contracted me to work for him. Over several years of doing business together, we established a great working relationship. Our values were very similar, we trusted each other, and we were both highly skilled at executing deliverables. I believe in collaborating and thought Mike would be an excellent person to collaborate with. So after winning a contract of $100,000 to provide leadership training to an organization where my point of contact had a $100 million operating budget, I thought Mike would be a good person to collaborate with. When I asked Mike if he had an interest, he enthusiastically said yes!

Mike and I had a conference call two nights before my meeting with the paying client. During the call with Mike, I covered the plan of action in detail. I shared with Mike a clear up-to-date, current status report of the classroom work and content that had been completed and delivered. I told Mike about my expectations of him, shared with him a few characteristics of the class participants, gave him an outline of the content we were to cover, and told Mike exactly what his role and responsibilities were going to be. I asked Mike if he had any questions. He had a few, which I answered.

On the day of the meeting with the customer, I started the work session, and everything was going well. I segued to Mike for his role that we had previously discussed. Mike took the handoff and transitioned seamlessly ... until he said "but." My ears immediately perked to attention and I was on high alert. After saying "but," Mike went into a spill of rhetoric that was beginning to lead the customer down a road we were not prepared to go down at the time. I interrupted Mike as if I were making a piggyback comment to his point, took over the presentation, and got us back on track.

When Mike and I convened in the parking lot after our work session, I asked Mike what led him to say "but," and then begin a discussion with the class that he and I had not talked about. Mike said he could see where I was taking the class, but thought they should be much further ahead. Mike conceded that he had made a mistake and that he had his own agenda in his mind.

This is one of the serious repercussions of collaboration and partnering. Sometimes we run into other people's hidden agendas. Needless to say, I was compelled to immediately dissolve any and all collaborative relationships with Mike. I could not let his hidden agenda jeopardize my contract and relationship with my client. The result? I kept doing business with my customer, and Mike and I are still friends.

One of the most successful periods I experienced in my consulting business was when I collaborated with two ladies over a period of three years. We were red hot during that time. All the stars were aligned. Values, expectations, skills, roles, responsibilities and personalities were all in synch. We were winning all the business that we went after.

The challenge came when we moved from collaborating to forming an official partnership. The minute we started to discuss revenue distribution, my team and I just could not get past how we were going to appropriately disburse money we hadn't even earned yet! There is no doubt what happened next. We crashed and burned, never to win another contract as a team.

The lesson I learned from that experience is that not all great collaborations will make great partnerships. Partnerships take a lot of work. Like a marriage, you and your partner will grow at different times. You must be willing to go through the peaks and valleys together at the same time, and it is important to recognize each other's strengths and growth areas and yield accordingly without blame or malice. When partnering, be sure to guard against the tendency to count your chicks before the eggs hatch. If you happen to catch yourself or your partner counting your chicks first, go back and review your "Why," the mission, and the Core Values. Check your egos at the door. Roll up your sleeves and begin to communicate by discussing, listening, and determining how decisions are going to be made that will guide the work to be completed.

Proceed with caution (but not fear) to take advantage of the opportunities, benefits and power that can come with Collaborating and Partnering. Always put forth the effort to complete your due diligence. It is a fact that more work can be accomplished with 10 good minds than with one genius mind. The 10 good minds will challenge the process from a variety of perspectives, resulting in several options that can be synthesized into greatness and genius.

The table on the next page can help you decide whether to collaborate or partner with someone depending on their vision, communication style and personality traits.

Collaborating	Partnering
Ability to resonate with your vision	Have a shared vision
Have similar to the same shared values	Have similar to the same shared values
Be acceptable to their role and responsibility	Take ownership of clear role and responsibility
Be able to see and feel your passion	Communicate without barriers
Contribute without prejudgment, malice or selfishness	Work without hidden agendas

Align yourself strategically with value-based Partnerships by having a definition and design of what an effective partnership will do for your business.

Whether based on a formal legal contract or an informal casual arrangement, those involved in Partnerships have a vested interest in profits and share in the costs and expenses of the business. The end game is very important to the partners. As we've seen, partners are often subject to hidden agendas. Most Partnerships are long term in tenure.

If you're considering establishing a business Partnership, take a few moments to answer the following questions:

What are the most important elements (knowledge, skills and experience) of a good Partnership for you?

1. _____

2. _____

3. _____

4. _____

Partnership Questions:
What are the values that you look for in a person or organization that will inspire you to MTA with them? Why?

_____

_____

_____

_____

_____

_____

_____

Align yourself strategically with value-based Collaborations. Having a definition and design of what an effective collaboration is for YOU will prove invaluable.

Collaborations are often formed when two or more people use an informal agreement, such as a Memorandum of

Understanding (MOU), or in some cases a simple handshake. The collaborative partners in many cases are contributing because they have very specific skills and/or resources to lend—most often their time—at a prorated cost or no cost at all. Most Collaborations are short term.

What are the most important elements (knowledge, skills and experience) of a good Collaboration for you?

1. _____

2. _____

3. _____

4. _____

Collaboration Questions:
What are the values that you look for in a person or organization that will inspire you to MTA with them? Why?

_____

_____

_____

_____

_____

_____

PRINCIPLE: VISION

D are	Dare to Dream! Dare to believe in what you imagine. Be Big, Bold, Audacious and Unstoppable.
R esearch	Dig to unearth the facts, data and statistics that support your endeavors.
E agle Eye	Sharpen your vision through Visualization, Meditation, Prayer and Faith.
A ssociates	Align yourself strategically with value-based Partnerships and Collaborations.
M entor	Accelerate your growth through Mentoring and Coaching.

Is there a difference between mentoring and collaborating? Ponder that question. Think back to our comments on collaborating. Remember, an emphasis was put on how others need to have similar values to yours and how important it is that others share your passion and vision. The collaborative direction is geared more toward you primarily, whereas in mentoring, the primary interest is with the other person, the person who you are mentoring, the mentee. Mentoring means putting your concern of another person's interests ahead of your own.

Why mentor? As you grow, learn, and gain accomplishment, it's important that your give back to others. Mentoring is a powerful relationship strategy that will offer a variety of benefits, not just for the mentee but for you, the mentor, as well. As the universe gives unto you, you surely should give back, and as you give back, you open yourself to be refilled. Part of having a laser sharp Vision is to reciprocate and care.

During your relationship with a mentee, you want to beware of the potential for slipping into "Coach Mode." Slipping into coach mode happens any time you challenge your mentee to perform a specific task and expect them to execute it within an agreed-upon timeframe. There is nothing wrong with using this coaching strategy while you are mentoring—as long as the mentee understands your intention. If the mentee does not recognize that you have moved into coach mode and thus does not respond to a challenge that you have issued, there is a high probability that ambiguous expectations may surface. With ambiguous expectations and misdirected actions—or lack of actions—the result can be confusion, lack of trust, and limited willingness.

If this type of situation materializes, the mentor-mentee relationship can begin to unravel. The goal is to create situations for the mentee to have a high probability for success. So be explicit with your expectations as you move forward in the relationship.

One way to create situations with a high probability of success for the mentee is to use what I call C3: clear, concise and compelling communication. In addition to listening without bias and prejudgment, you want to be clear about your expectations.

There are six types of expectations to know about. These expectations are used with great frequency. When expectations are established incorrectly, carelessly or with malicious intent, they will hurt and destroy. However, when expectations are established properly, with care and understanding, they will create amazing outcomes.

The six expectations are very easy to remember. They are: Known, Spoken, Realistic, Unknown, Unspoken, and Unrealistic. It's the Unknown, Unspoken and Unrealistic expectations that most often cause the issues. Holding a person accountable to one of the Un-expectations is a sure way to create chaos, misunderstanding and resentment.

Just as important, when you are mentoring, pay attention to conversation cues like framing, context, body language, tone and word usage when delivering and receiving a message. The goal throughout your mentoring conversations is to have great clarity so that being held accountable is a non-issue.

I remember as a freshman in college, I decided I was going to major in Business Economics. The course work was a little challenging for me. Then one day while in the gym playing basketball with my new friend Cedric, I received a blessing and a curse. (Okay, maybe not a curse.) After Cedric and I were done playing basketball, we headed back across the campus to our dorm. As we walked and talked, the blessing came. I discovered that Cedric was a Business Econ major. I shared with Cedric that I was majoring in the exact same subject but that I was struggling.

Cedric told me the subject came very easily to him. He even offered to tutor me. His gesture was outstanding! I was smiling from ear to ear. After a few sessions of Cedric mentoring and tutoring me, my academic life began to get better. But then, as fate would have it, one day Cedric came into the TV room in our dorm. He had a huge smile on his face and exclaimed that he had great news. Cool, I thought. I couldn't wait to hear what he had to say. Lo and behold, Cedric said, "I got the job that I have been working so hard to land."

"Congratulations," I remarked. "Where is the job located?"

"I'm headed to Texas," said Cedric. "I will be leaving in December right after graduation."

Graduation! December! Leaving! What? This was not making sense to me. It was October. How in the heck was he leaving in December? I asked Cedric, "But what about you mentoring me and our tutoring sessions? How will I survive?" Cedric did his best to console me. Cedric told me that I was smart, that he had great confidence in me, and that he could see me beginning to understand the concepts with more ease.

He told me that he had a couple of people he could refer me to for tutoring. Cedric went on to explain to me that he was a graduate student finishing up his last semester and that he would be graduating in December. Selfishly, I asked Cedric if he could stay for one more semester. Of course, that answer was NO. Cedric was a great mentor for me. However, because we did not give attention to addressing all of my expectations as the mentee, I ended up being disappointed with the end result of our mentoring relationship.

So back to the drawing board. I changed my major to Occupational Safety and Health Engineering, earned my Bachelor of Science degree, and learned a lot about expectations. As a mentor and mentee, I always keep the six expectations in the forefront of my mind, right next to my values and my "Why." This practice has proven to be tremendously beneficial for me more often than not.

Mentoring involves developing a relationship of sharing, caring and great communication. As you continue to grow in prosperity and abundance, be sure to give of your gift. Pursue mentoring with a stated vision, mission, outline, ground rules and established expectations for how you and your mentee will operate. Make mentoring natural, intentional and purposeful. You will enjoy the fun and reap a ton of rewards, like self-fulfillment, self-awareness, discovery, new relationships, new business, and new contacts. All of these benefits and rewards help contribute to sharpening your Vision.

When you mentor, you give of yourself unselfishly. Why? Because you CARE. MTA with C.A.R.E:

- ☐ **C**oncern – Put others' interests first.

- ☐ **A**ttentive – Listen without judgment, prejudgment or bias.

- ☐ **R**espect – Do not operate solely from assumption, over-confidence, or familiarity. Dig, dig, dig to learn more.

- ☐ **E**nergy – Work to MTA with the proper rest, exercise, and nutrition.

When contemplating your mentoring strategy, approach and target audience, consider these questions:

1. Think of people or an organization whom you know or suspect of having a similar "Why?" as your own. What is their "Why"?

2. Think of someone or an organization with similar values as yours. What are their Values?

3. Think of someone or an organization with whom you would be willing to share your knowledge, wisdom and experiences with as a mentor. Describe your reason. Why?

CHAPTER 5

STRATEGY

Strategy: The art of devising a plan of action to achieve an objective or goal.

Walt Disney started his first Disney studio with his brother Roy in the early 1920s. Walt Disney would create short cartoon films with voice and then he would synchronize sound to enhance his product. Film was always Disney's choice. Disney believed that a cartoon feature film would be more profitable and so he premiered "Snow White and the Seven Dwarfs" in 1937 after four years of work. In 1957, Disney sketched out an image depicting his core business as grounded in films, with a portfolio of entertainment assets (theme parks, cartoons, magazines, commercials, business films, publications and merchandise) supported and reinforced by the movies. Today, the Walt Disney Company uses the same strategic premise with an evolved strategic process that involves parallel thinking to

analyze a problem, generate ideas, evaluate ideas, and then construct and critique a plan of action. This process works to create and refine its strategic plan.

Think of Strategy characteristically like a Fox. The Fox is detailed, meticulous and crafty. Consistently in "thoughts developed" mode, the Fox is organized and strategic; he's also tough to keep up with because he's so competitive.

Most of us have room to improve in our personal and professional lives. Whatever can be improved can also be measured, and through measurement you can evaluate your return on investment. Strategizing is an effective technique of planning and directing operations and movements to accomplish an end goal.

As a football player from the age of 15 years old through my senior year in college, I have always been under the direction of great strategists who coached me to achieve at high levels. I recognized the importance and rewards of strategic planning and execution at every level of football that I played, starting with: Junior League travel team, Tomahawks National Champions, Dick Sietz; Woodward High School, Public High School Champions, Jack Campbell; Murray State University, Ohio Valley Conference Champions, Mike Gottfried, Frank Beamer and Ron Zook.

The strategic way of winning and being a champion was instilled deep in my DNA so much that when I entered the workforce after college, I only chose to work for those companies who were the best in their industry, like Kroger, LensCrafters, Terminix and Sysco. While functioning in management capacity with operating statement responsibility for up to $30,000,000 while also providing leadership to teams of up to 300 people, strategy was key to my success in corporate America.

At Kroger I wrote the strategy for the company to implement an annual food show exposition. The initiative increased sales, in-store customer count, brand recognition and brand awareness. With LensCrafters I designed and implemented a strategic inventory process that produced the fastest in-store inventory count at that time. The process reduced store loss and increased profits. With Sysco I designed and implemented an inventory and communication strategy that was used for the buildouts of a chain of chicken restaurants called Boston Chicken (Market) that was duplicated nationally. With Terminix I developed a strategic Customer Relations Management system that provided a platform for a newly created commercial division to open communication channels for sales and service to an expanding client list.

Strategy has always been a part of my life. Without documented strategic processes, I do not believe I would have been able to live the life of a champion or been as successful at my endeavors. I have been blessed to learn from some of the best coaches, mentors, and business leaders in the country. Now I am ready to share with you what I have learned. The process that I am going to share is simple yet powerful. But first, there are a few things you should know.

Writing effective strategy that leverages position of achievement can be tough. Too often, people plan, set and follow through on multiple strategies throughout the day without ever writing them down, formally or informally. I'm sure that you have awakened and said something like; "Today I'm going to do yard work, go to the grocery store and do the laundry before my favorite show comes on at 4:30 p.m." Or how about, "I am going to meet with my collaborative stakeholders today and then I am going to finish my report that is due by 5:00 p.m." Sound familiar? Pretty decent everyday strategies, right?

The problem is that when you task yourself with actions that weren't previously documented with a strategic process, you can't expect to achieve at your highest capacity. Often those kinds of informal or verbal strategic actions get clumped together with other actions that aren't as important and then uh oh! Something gets left out because there is no accountability and the excuses are right around the corner. Have you been there before? Most of us have!

This is why strategic plans need to be written down. Writing is the mother of all repetition. Repetition develops consistency. Consistency builds discipline. So writing out your strategy consistently can be very effective, especially when you frame your strategy with the following core elements:

- a stated objective
- accountability measures
- a timeline
- a reference point
- an incentive to act

How you move about in your day-to-day operations, the media that you use to communicate across functions, and the actions you take to implement effective and efficient strategic processes do not have to be complex or cumbersome. The complexity is going to come in doing the work. So keep your strategy simple, straightforward and process-oriented.

Without further delay, I introduce a powerful strategic process that I have fallen in love with: OGSM. OGSM is an easy-to-implement framework that will assist you with contextualizing your strategy. In the CDIS model, where

Strategy is listed as the third principle, the supporting process is OGSM.

OGSM is a technique with roots dating back to Japan in the 1950s during the occupation post-World War II. OGSM has been adopted by many Fortune 500 companies—most notably Proctor and Gamble. As a global company, Proctor and Gamble uses OGSM across their entire enterprise. In addition to Proctor and Gamble, many consultants have begun to use the OGSM framework in their practice as well.

The OGSM framework forms the basis for strategic planning and execution. It also functions as a strong management tool that keeps your plan in sight, relevant and active in your day-to-day operations. Spelled out, OGSM is straightforward and simple: O-Objectives, G-Goals, S-Strategies, and M-Measures.

Illustrated on the following page is OGSM as a working frame.

OGSM FRAMEWORK

WHAT		HOW	
OBJECTIVES	GOALS	STRATEGIES	MEASURES
ASPIRATION	QUANTITATIVE TARGET	ACTIONS	OUTPUTS
What you want to achieve	Quantitative articulation of the objective	Key priorities and actions; what you will do to meet the objective	Measures that tell whether strategies are meeting goals
WORDS	NUMBERS	WORDS	NUMBERS
The Strategies should achieve the Objective, and the Measures should tell if your Strategies are achieving your Goals.			

Chart 8

When stating your Objectives, you want to construct them as broad, overreaching statements describing the essence of your expected outcome. Your Goals are best written for the purpose of moving to action and should be written deliberately to be specific, measurable, achievable, results-oriented, and completed within a specified timeframe. Strategy will describe how you are going to manage the distribution and allocation of resources, while Measures will provide a peek into your progress and effectiveness by using key process indicators and milestones as your feedback loop.

Following is a case study that will help you see the OGSM framework in action:

A long-time coaching client of mine in the construction business was in a fog. After talking to the coaching client and riding with him on several of his calls, I noticed he was missing his confidence and seemed to have little to no structure for his work day and work week. The client was extremely knowledgeable, his customers and prospective clients loved him, and he had plenty of opportunity to grow his business. After extensive conversation with my coaching client, we mapped out the following OGSM in the form of a narrative and later as a dashboard.

<u>*Objective*</u> – To provide quality and on-time service that exceeds the customer's expectations.

<u>*Goals*</u> – Construct one weekly work schedule on the Sunday prior to the beginning of a work week. Construct five days per week with daily specific work schedules the day prior to the actual work day. Every Saturday, Monday and Wednesday, allocate three hours for preparing and reviewing contract proposals. Target timeframes: Sat. and Mon. 6:30 – 9:30 a.m. and Wed. 6:00 – 9:00 p.m.

<u>*Strategies*</u> – On weekly schedules, identify suppliers, customers, and trades to contact for upcoming work flow. Identify materials to be ordered and where to be distributed to

determine workload. On daily schedules, determine time to contact specific people. Determine route per priority.

Measures – Are contract proposals completed on time? Is there a daily work schedule for every week?

WHAT		HOW	
OBJECTIVES	GOALS	STRATEGIES	MEASURES
Provide quality on-time service, exceed customer's expectation	Wkly. Sched. 1 day before work week Write detailed sched. 5 days/wk. 3 days/wk. review proposals	ID suppliers, cust. and trades Comprise order list and workload Prioritize call list and daily route	Contract proposal complete on or before deadline 4 Weekly sched. every month Productive days are equal/greater than 90% complete
WORDS	NUMBERS	WORDS	NUMBERS
The strategies should achieve the objective and the measures should tell you if your strategies are achieving your goals.			

Chart 9

After implementation of the strategy, monthly follow-up, and nine months of coaching, the client expressed it took him 30 – 45 days to get fully on track. Once fully on track, the client expressed that he had regained his confidence, his energy level had increased, and he had seen an increase in revenue. The client also expressed that where he previously was always behind on contract proposals, he had seen a dramatic improvement and was more prepared to take on multiple jobs with confidence as he managed his budget more efficiently. When I first met the client, he was literally all shook up. However, after this exercise, the client says he will always use OGSM.

How about you? Will you use OGSM? Check out the OGSM process in further detail on the following pages and apply OGSM to a project you are working on—or perhaps to a vacation that you are planning—and see how easy, how productive, and how efficient OGSM makes your life.

PRINCIPLE: STRATEGY

O bjectives	Construct a broad statement describing the essence of your expected outcome.
G oals	
S trategy	
M easures	

Objective *(Words)* – Your objective is a broad overreaching statement to indicate what is critical or important to accomplish. Objective is the target expectation of accomplishment.

Examples:

- For family vacation, my family and I plan to travel 30 days along the Eastern Coastline.

- Introduce existing products into a new market.

- To continually learn and adopt current best practices.

- Decrease company expenses by 5%.

Practice writing a few of your own Objective statements:

1. _____

_____

_____

_____

2. _____

_____

_____

_____

3. _____

_____

_____

_____

PRINCIPLE: STRATEGY

O bjectives	Construct a broad statement describing the essence of your expected outcome.
G oals	Write your goal to be Specific, Measurable, Achievable, Results-Oriented, and completed within a defined Time Frame.
S trategy	
M easures	

Goals (*Numbers*) – Write the elements of your goal deliberately to be SMART. Goals are the driving force in helping you work toward accomplishing the Objective.

Examples: *Reduce raw material inventory levels from 31 days average to 23 days average with a maximum of 27 days by August 1, 2020. The management team will take the lead beginning August 1, 2019. The project evaluation will extend until December 31, 2020.*

Write a practice Goal.

_____

_____

_____

_____

_____

_____

_____

_____

_____

_____

_____

_____

_____

_____

_____

_____

_____

_____

_____

_____

Now write the same goal in S.M.A.R.T segments.

Specific – detailed description, not broad

Measurable – must have two points (a beginning and an end)

Achievable – resources are available and accessible; expectations are known, spoken, and realistic

Results-Oriented – use verbs to inspire action and account-ability

Time Frame – a period of time during which an activity is to take place

Now combine the segments and write a clear, concise, and compelling SMART GOAL.

_____

_____

_____

_____

_____

_____

_____

_____

_____

_____

_____

_____

_____

_____

_____

_____

_____

_____

_____

_____

_____

PRINCIPLE: STRATEGY

O bjectives	Construct a broad statement describing the essence of your expected outcome.
G oals	Write your goal to be Specific, Measurable, Achievable, Results-Oriented, and completed within a defined Time Frame.
S trategy	Describe how you are going to manage the distribution and allocation of resources.
M easures	

Strategy (*Words*) – Describe how you are going to manage the distribution and allocation of resources. Strategy is how you achieve the Goals that are the drivers for accomplishing the Objective.

For an approach to effectively and efficiently write the strategy narrative, use the following set of questions:

- **What?**

  Objective Questions — They invite sharing and build consciousness. They generate options and possibilities. Brainstorm and identify possible solutions.

- **Now What?**

  Decisional Questions — They develop opinions / options / solutions that lead to future actions. They clarify expectations for improvement or change.

- **So What?**

  Interpretive Questions — They invite parallel thinking and solicit alternative feedback to reduce the possibility of operating with blind spots.

- **Then What?**

  Reflective Questions — They elicit emotional response and personal reactions. They invite a deepened level of participation: think, feel, believe, gauge.

- **What might I be missing?**

  After asking and answering the line of *what* questions as they relate to your goals and objective, practice writing a few strategies. Remember, strategies are the narrative for how you are going to achieve goals.

Describe your Strategy …

PRINCIPLE: STRATEGY

O bjectives	Construct a broad statement describing the essence of your expected outcome.
G oals	Write your goal to be Specific, Measurable, Achievable, Results-Oriented, and completed within a defined Time Frame.
S trategy	Describe how you are going to manage the distribution and allocation of resources.
M easures	Use Key Performance Indicators and Milestones for feedback on strategy implementation.

Measures should tell you if your Strategies are working. Measures are stated with numbers and can be determined by using Key Performance Indicators (KPIs) and Milestones. Think of your KPIs and Milestones as your feedback loop. Without proper and good reliable feedback, you are at risk of doing what you have always done, expecting different results, but getting the same results (if not worse).

KPIs are a type of performance measurement that help to understand how your organization, team or department is performing with regards to strategy implementation.

An effective KPI will exhibit the following qualities:

☐ Be well defined and quantifiable

☐ Be well communicated to individuals, teams, groups, departments, divisions, etc.

☐ Be crucial to achieving your strategy (hence, *key* performance indicators)

☐ Be applicable to your Line of Business (LOB), department, division or branch

Example: If you sell display ad space on your website, and display banner advertisement as a source of revenue on your website, you might define a KPI around the subject of how many page views you generate in 90 days and then compare +/- page views versus previous 90 days.

What are three KPIs for a project that you are currently involved in?

1. _____

2. _____

3. _____

A Milestone is a specific point in time with a beginning date and an end date. Use Milestones to determine if your Strategies are working.

Example: Project Start Date August 1, 2018

Milestone	Due Date	Who's Responsible	Details
Reconfigure Social Media Account	February 5, 2019	Jimmy Taylor	Research best practice
Social Media Program	March 15, 2019	Ann Mitchell	Everyone on same page

Milestones are used as signal posts for:

☐ A project's start and/or end date

☐ A need for external review or input

☐ A need for budget checks

☐ A submission of a major deliverable

☐ and much more

Milestones have a fixed date but no duration.

What are three Milestones for a work/project that you are involved in?

1. _____

2. _____

3. _____

CHAPTER 6

BRANDING

Branding: To differentiate with consistency and dependability your features, advantages and benefits for the customer's value proposition.

Born into poverty, a child was born to an unmarried teenager who worked as a maid. Throughout the child's youth years, she was shuffled back and forth between relatives and schools, always living in poverty. The girl was molested for years by family members. Things began to turn around for the child at the age of 17, after winning a statewide competition. A local radio station took notice and hired the teenager to do news part-time. That started the teenager's career in media. In 1978, the news reporter was recruited to co-host a local Baltimore talk show called "People Are Talking." (If you guessed that this person is Oprah Winfrey, then you guessed correctly.) In 1983, Oprah moved to Chicago where she took over a morning show

called "AM Chicago," and within months took it from last place to first in the city! Three years later, "The Oprah Winfrey Show" was born. Oprah popularized and revolutionized the tabloid talk show genre pioneered by Phil Donahue. She reinvented her show with a focus on literature, self-improvement, mindfulness and spirituality. In 2008, she formed her own network, Oprah Winfrey Network (OWN), and she has never looked back.

Think of Branding characteristically like a Giraffe. The Giraffe is bold and strong with a stature that literally stands out among all others. With superb vision, speed, power and discipline, the Giraffe moves gracefully and purposefully.

Do you remember when only celebrities and major companies had personal brands? Actors, musicians, Fortune 100 businesses, and athletes got all the attention. All of that has changed now. There is competition in all that we do.

Branding is the fourth principle in CDIS, and it refers to your Personal Brand. This principle of Personal Branding is too often overlooked. In this chapter, I will share with you what I know about Personal Branding and introduce you to the SING process.

A brand is something you are constantly building because it is the affirmation of who you are and what you love to do.

When I talk about Personal Branding, I am referring to establishing and promoting what you stand for. Your personal brand is the unique combination of skills and experiences that you possess. Effective personal branding will differentiate you from others, from your competition, and help you stand out from the crowd.

Professionally, think about your work performance, how you are evaluated in your work, and your skill set. Personally, think about your personality, your character, and your physical presence. These are many of the traits that people evaluate and assess when they engage with you. If you are not consciously and cognitively taking control of your narrative—i.e., what you want others to know about you and how you want to influence the way others think about you—then others will take complete control of "branding" you. When others take control of your brand narrative, you are going to have an uphill battle. If the way other people have branded you is not in alignment with your Core Values and doesn't connect to your "Why," it could be extremely damaging. Do I have your attention?

It's essential that you care about and cultivate your Personal Brand. You are unique, special, talented, capable and gifted with skill. These are attributes that create a difference between you and everyone else. The way you deliver your work, your consistency, your quality, your durability, dependability and value are how people will judge you and perceive you. The good news is that the Personal Branding phenomenon is nothing new. In some form or fashion, you have been practicing Personal Branding for some time. What has changed is the amount of competition.

According to an *HR Daily Advisor* article, "How to Handle 5 Generations in the Workplace,"[1] today there are five generations of people in the workforce at the same time. You have the **Traditionalists** born before 1946, **Baby Boomers** born between 1946-1964, **Generation X** born between 1965-1976, **Generation Y** or **Millennials** born between 1977-1997, and **Generation Z** born after 1997. This generational mix creates a very dynamic interaction and vibrant competition among people.

When you are in competition, most often you want to shine. You want to stand out beyond the others. This is where Personal Branding can give you the edge in your personal and/or professional life. To convey my strategies of Personal Branding with you, I am going to share a few stories, give an overview of the SING process, and finally cover SING step by step.

As a performance consultant who provides human capital solutions and facilitates leadership and communication

---

[1] Lin Grensing-Pophal, Feb. 26, 2019

strategies, I have plenty of competition to contend with. In this industry, relationships, reputation, connectivity and execution are huge deciding factors in who wins the business. The competition is fierce. For me, this is where I benefit once again from my training as an athlete and as an accomplished and experienced manager in corporate America. In both college football and in corporate America, what I heard over and over again like the beat of a rhythmic drum were phrases like, "Stand out amongst the crowd," "leave your footprint," and "do good things so people will know good things about you." The message to me was all about personal branding. Build your brand, execute on your brand promise, protect your brand, and always stay true to your brand.

My biggest strength, and a key component to my Personal Brand, is my ability to execute. Upon entering into a contract with a new customer, I listen to what my customer's wants are, I get clarity of their expectation, I share with them a proposed solution and an implementation strategy, I get their buy-in, and then I go execute. I do not miss a step in the process. I do not take the process for granted. The reason I am so deliberate in this process is because it is the underpinning of my brand. The combination of my brand and my process are what allow me to retain existing customers for additional business and also secure referrals for prospective new customers.

I have a long-time customer who gave me one of my first shots at earning their business and executing their stated objective. That relationship has grown for more than 15 years and I have penetrated almost every business unit in their organization. Penetration as a mode of personal branding has been a true anchor for the tenure of my business.

Following the SING process will make it easy for you to get started with building and refining your Personal Brand. As you build and/or refine your brand, your mere presence will begin to shine brightly, reflecting that you are living your best life. Let your brand shine.

There is an old saying that goes, "music soothes the savage beast." Music can be tranquil, spiritual and inspiring. So why not SING about your Personal Brand? Creating the difference that distinguishes you from others involves identifying your Strengths. Although somewhere on this earth there is someone who looks very similar to you, one of the most miraculous events ever is that we have all been created differently.

What attracts others to you is your magnetic quality. You want to accentuate your magnetic quality as your Intentional Acts. Every day is full of new experiences which add to your story. Everyone has a different story to tell about what makes them different, and your story is your Necessary Message. Yet in order to stay at the top of your game, you will always want to be open to receive feedback, learn and improve. That's called Growth.

The more you practice and work to build and/or refine your Brand, you will see how it complements anything and everything you do. Simply doing this one thing could be the capstone of your authenticity and the catalyst to living your best life.

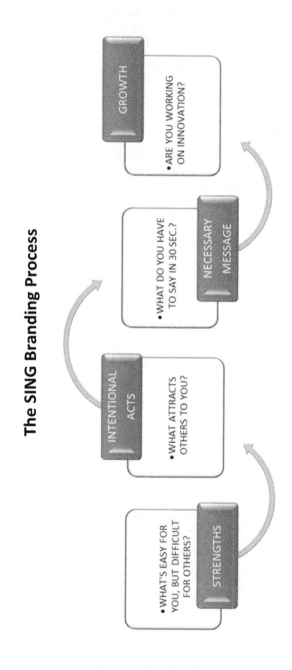

The SING Branding Process

GROWTH
• ARE YOU WORKING ON INNOVATION?

NECESSARY MESSAGE
• WHAT DO YOU HAVE TO SAY IN 30 SEC.?

INTENTIONAL ACTS
• WHAT ATTRACTS OTHERS TO YOU?

STRENGTHS
• WHAT'S EASY FOR YOU, BUT DIFFICULT FOR OTHERS?

PRINCIPLE: BRANDING

S trengths	Identify three to five attributes that differentiate your offering from those of your competitors.
I ntentional Acts	
N ecessary Message	
G rowth	

Branding is the practice of creating a name, symbol or design that identifies and differentiates one product from other products. "Products" are defined as anything that can be offered to satisfy a want or need, including physical goods, services, experiences, events, places, properties, organizations, information, ideas and persons.

A product can be easily copied by other players in a market, but a brand should always be unique. For example, Pepsi and Coca-Cola taste very similar; however, some people feel more connected to Coca-Cola, and others to Pepsi. That's because both brands are unique.

In very simple words, a product is what you sell, a brand is the perceived image of the product you sell, and branding is the strategy to create that image. Your brand is largely made up by your Value Proposition. Your Value Proposition is what you promise of value to be communicated and acknowledged. It is also the belief and expectation held by customers and prospective clients about the value they expect to receive by doing business with you. Your special skill sets, experiences and personality are key attributes in the makeup of your value proposition.

What are three to five of your strongest differentiating attributes (strengths) that support your value proposition?

Examples of differentiating attributes (strengths) from Coca-Cola include: *taste, happiness, logo, the real thing, Santa Claus, hope, family, love, gifts, fun*

1. _____

2. _____

3. _____

4. _____

5. _____

You should feel really good about your three to five differentiating attributes. As a matter of fact, your differentiating attributes should tie directly to your "Why." If you need to think about your differentiating attributes one more time, or review them one more time, do that right now. Ensure that you *own* your differentiating attributes and that they really distinguish you.

Having understanding, knowledge and awareness about who you are, inside and out, speaks to your self-concept. When you know your self-concept and move within your core values, your confidence grows. As your confidence grows, your next move will be compelling with magnetic intentional acts.

PRINCIPLE: BRANDING

S trengths	Identify three to five attributes that differentiate your offering from those of your competitors.
I ntentional Acts	Identify your compelling actions that resonate with others.
N ecessary Message	
G rowth	

Intentional Acts are behaviors, actions, language and presentation that you move with daily. During interpersonal communication, the messages that you communicate are first - in your mind, second - in your body language, third - in your tone, and fourth - in your words.

Studies by Dr. Albert Mehrabian, Professor Emeritus of Psychology at UCLA, have shown that generally, on a 100% scale, the interpersonal messages you convey are received by others as follows:

Body language	55%
Tone	38%
Words	7%

People will form an opinion about you within the first 90 seconds after seeing and hearing you. Next, they will spend three to five minutes affirming their initial thoughts about you.

You can have direct influence on how you resonate with others and how they resonate with you. How you resonate with others is based on four things: (1) things you know about yourself, (2) things others know about you that they *tell* you, (3) things others know about you but *don't* tell you, and (4) things you don't know about yourself and others don't know about you, either. The first three are what you want to focus on immediately. Take time to get feedback from others in addition to what you already know.

Take a few moments now to journal your thoughts in the spaces on the following pages. It is important that you are knowledgeable and aware of the persona you project, the situational body language you exhibit and how your language and tone impact others so you can articulate with influence and MTA with confidence.

Identify your compelling actions that resonate with others and consistently MTA relentlessly.

_____

_____

_____

_____

_____

_____

_____

What actions, tasks, behaviors, and performances are you better at than most?

_____

_____

_____

_____

_____

_____

_____

What skills, techniques and knowledge have you refined to mastery level better than most?

_____
_____
_____
_____
_____
_____
_____

Next, brainstorm and record some of your greatest successes and life lessons. Once you are done, put initials next to items on the list that reflect what you do best and what attracts people to you.

_____
_____
_____
_____
_____
_____

Finally, construct a short list or a brief paragraph describing your compelling Intentional Acts:

Use the following initials to identify what you do best: t-task; b-behaviors; p-performance; s-skills; tq-techniques; and k-knowledge.

PRINCIPLE: BRANDING

S trengths	Identify three to five attributes that differentiate your offering from those of your competitors.
I ntentional Acts	Identify your compelling actions that resonate with others.
N ecessary Message	Identify who you are, what service you provide, and what problem you solve.
G rowth	

Upon an initial meeting, people form opinions of one another within the first 30-90 seconds.

- First communication = your thoughts
- Second communication = your body language
- Third communication = your tone
- Fourth communication = your words

A 30-second elevator pitch or sound bite will often work to your benefit and increase your value. Write and practice your 30-second elevator pitch or sound bite. Work to be certain that your pitch provides good context for your message, your content is relevant to your audience, and your words and language are C3 (Clear, Concise and Compelling).

Be sure to include:

- who you are;

- what service you provide; and

- what problem you solve.

Consider incorporating recent accomplishments, relevant industry specifics, special collaboration or partnership relationships, specialized training, etc.

PRINCIPLE: BRANDING

S trengths	Identify three to five attributes that differentiate your offering from those of your competitors.
I ntentional Acts	Identify your compelling actions that resonate with others.
N ecessary Message	Identify who you are, what service you provide, and what problem you solve.
G rowth	Assess and determine for innovation the value of your product and/or service.

Growth is the process of increasing—either in amount, value or importance. To ensure Growth, a feedback loop is critical.

A feedback loop will show you what areas you need to work on for self-improvement and strengthening your Branding. You can create a feedback loop by connecting with existing customers, past clients, friends, family, or even your spouse.

When selecting people to include in your Feedback Loop, it's best to:

- Seek someone with expert knowledge in your aspiring growth area, with similar values to yours, and who is a good communicator.

- Create scenarios strategically to get feedback around the subjects of your work, project, team, collaboration, etc.

- Choose a topic with relevant content, frame it with context, and integrate a survey.

Common subjects that you might want to request feedback about include:

- Am I reliable?
- Are my products durable?
- Is the quality consistent?
- Am I dependable?
- Am I delivering on my Value Proposition?

Of course, feedback on its own does nothing unless you're committed to acting upon it for Growth. So be sure to ask yourself the following questions:

- What are you going to do with the feedback?
- What type of feedback are you targeting to receive?
- What method(s) are you going to use to manage your feedback?

Remember, your Brand is your new business card. When designed and delivered well, your Brand will precede you, it will differentiate you, and it will assist you in gaining access. Always continue to refine your Brand and deliver it with confidence.

CONCLUSION

Writing this book has been a great journey for me. In many ways, the work was easy because I developed the content from a desire to be great and to be recognized as a world thought leader. My mission is and always has been to share information with people so they are more informed to make better decisions to improve the quality of their personal and professional life. In some ways, writing this book was also quite difficult. Like most writers, I struggled with negative experiences like fatigue, wanting to be done, writer's block, not wanting to read another page, and lack of confidence.

What really inspired me to push through to the finish line was the constant support that I received from family, friends, prayers, faith, and passion. Complete. The book is now done. Living in the moment, I am realizing that my path on this journey is widening. I see a brighter light on the horizon, and my responsibility is to stay true and authentic with the message that I am charged to deliver.

One of my favorite mantras that guides my energy is, "It is not *about* me, it's *because* of me." What this means to me is that I have to be selfless when I am interacting with others. Being selfless puts me in a position to be of service. I have to be humble. For me, being humble means relinquishing my ego so that I'm not perceived by others as dominating or intimidating.

I have to be inclusive. I believe inclusiveness is a charge for me to learn, investigate and dig, dig, dig about the people, places or situations that I am going to be a part of in order for the collective of us to achieve greater results.

I have to be aware of my emotions. Emotions are fleeting and should not be depended upon as a tool to make decisions. I must be aware of how my emotions play into my decisions and understand that accountability is a consequence.

"It is not *about* me, it's *because* of me."

I know my charge as I move forward from this milestone. My question for you is, do you know your charge? Have you found a new charge? Are you thinking about new and different endeavors?

Coaching Dreams Into Success is all about you living your best life. Why not you? Why not right now?

Be decisive in what you choose to do and how you plan to take action. Do not let misfortune or setbacks put you in a sedentary position. You will have challenges and successes; that is a known fact. Remember, it's okay to go to the pity party—just don't stay there too long. It's okay to celebrate, too—just don't stay there too long, either. My daughter once gave me a quote from Dennis Kimbro that I will share with you: "Your birth is evidence that your purpose is necessary."

It is imperative for you to reach out into the universe of positive people who share similar to the same values as yours, take the time to ground yourself so you can see the forest from the trees, and infiltrate your mind with positive constructs versus the want of insignificant material objects and intentional prohibiting messages. Don't be afraid to be the true change—the real change—that you want to create. Explore and develop your greatness.

As you continue working with the principles from *Coaching Dreams Into Success*, your Balance, Vision, Strategy and Branding will be held in the forefront of your thoughts. Implementing and practicing the processes of EVAL, DREAM, OGSM, and SING will assist you with navigating, leveraging and winning your way to the finish line of whatever your pursuit may be.

I am very appreciative for your purchase of this book. Thank you! Are you open to sharing a success that CDIS helped you realize? I would love to hear from you and learn about your story. Visit my website at CoachingDreamsIntoSuccess.com and give me a shout.

Index

Made in the USA
Monee, IL
26 March 2022

93046849R00089